DATE DUE

DEMCO 38-296

Cheer Up...
You're Only Half Dead

Cheer Up...

You're Only Half Dead

Reflections at Mid-Life

Robin T.W. Yuan, M.D.

Prometheus Books
59 John Glenn Drive
Amherst, New York 14228-2197

To my father and mother

Published 1996 by Prometheus Books

00 99 98 97 96   5 4 3 2 1

Library of Congress Cataloging-in-Publication Data

Yuan, Robin T. W.
    Cheer up—you're only half dead! : reflections at mid-life / Robin T. W. Yuan, M.D.
        p.   cm.
    ISBN 1–57392–078–9 (cloth : alk. paper)
    1. Middle age—United States. 2. Middle aged persons—United States—Psychology. I. Title.
HQ1059.5.U5Y83   1996
305.24′4—dc20
                                                                                96–22611
                                                                                CIP

Printed in the United States of America on acid-free paper

Contents

Introduction

Christmas 1990 was a typical, blistering cold day in Boston, when the air bites at the skin and each breath stings the lungs. I had just arrived from my home in sunny California for our traditional year-end family reunion. The heavy, wet snow quickly melted on my face, each flake prickling as it landed. I shook my father's powerful hand, thinking how he looked shorter this year than last. After a brief and quiet ride from the airport, I soon stood in the dry warmth of my cozy bedroom in Newton, steam forcing its way through the hissing floor pipes, where, three decades ago, I had listened to the Boston Red Sox broadcasts on my cheap transistor radio smuggled into bed under the protection of my pillow much too late on a school night. The radio was Japanese-made. And I remembered that, in those days, we knew that nothing good was ever made in Japan.

In this very bedroom I had practiced shooting my tee shirts at light fixtures perched at either end of the small room, pretending I was John Havilcek of the world-champion Boston Celtics. I looked around at the sturdy wooden desk in the corner of the room where I had spent many a dark and lonely night hunched over my mother's ancient light microscope, the one she had used during her medical school days at the University of Pennsylvania forty years before. I studied leaves, fingernails, semen—anything I could. In my impossibly short twin bed, which barely contained my full adult length, I had read *Johnny Tremain* and Edgar Rice Burroughs's *Tarzan of the Apes,* learned geometry and the meaning of exponential powers.

Now I looked into the mirror mounted on my boy-sized bureau. Poised to blow-dry my hair following a much-needed bath, I suddenly realized that I had to stoop to two-thirds my height in order to see my own face. As a teenager, I had always thought I was bigger than most of my classmates. Today I saw how small I really was back then. It hurt my spine to hold this position in front of the mirror. My neck ached and my back cracked with all the bending. Even as I took great care to gently comb my hair, hair fell out with ease. I tried to avoid blow-drying the roots, which were so delicate and precious. And when I directed the heated stream of air above my high, proud forehead, I could see clearly— too clearly—my scalp shining through the thinning strands.

The average life span for a white male (although technically speaking I'm not *white*-white) is seventy-two years. I was thirty-six and a half that Christmas of 1990. My father was fast approaching seventy. Night had fallen before the afternoon was out, for the days were the shortest this time of year. And so, hands held motionless above my head for that poignant moment of inspiration, the house quiet with reflection, I stared at my present, my face no longer resembling the roly-poly young kid with the bristly crew-cut. My joints aching and my belly soft, I thought a frighteningly funny thought. Here I was, a Harvard graduate twice over, a prominent Beverly Hills plastic surgeon, a former childhood genius, near musical prodigy . . . half dead!

1

Sport Scores

Like most boys growing up in Boston, or anywhere in America, I loved sports. Every kid had his favorite team and mine was the Boston Red Sox. Baseball was the all-American sport. Boys of all ages played baseball in every sandlot, country field, and city street across America, and dreamed of becoming major leaguers. Trying out real leather gloves at Sears or picking out your first bat with your hero's authentic autograph burnt into the ash wood were memorable events. I loved opening the box of a brand-new baseball and rubbing the shine off the cowhide, turning a simple toy into a lifetime of memories. Little else mattered to young boys but baseball.

Despite a well-deserved reputation for choking down the home stretch, the Red Sox—no matter how bad, no matter how far behind the pack—were always number one with me. Winning, while important, wasn't everything. The optimism, the social renaissance, of the post-war years seemed to infect even the smallest of sportsmen. I always believed it when they said, "Wait'll next year!"

There was nothing like baseball, Beantown, and boyhood in the 1960s.

■ ■ ■

I remember entering revered Fenway Park in 1960 with its Green Mon-ster wall towering thirty-seven feet above left field. A ball walloped over the twenty-three-foot net at the top of the wall could land in an open-bed truck on the Massachusetts Turnpike and travel all the way to Oklahoma. Fenway had one of the few true bullpens that was built between the right field fence and the wide-open bleacher seats beyond it. The Red Sox bullpen stood back to back with the visitor's bullpen. Any batted ball sail-ing over the fence and caught by a relief pitcher while warming up in this bullpen was a home run, causing the players in the bullpen to cheer or swear depending on whose bullpen it had landed in. Beyond the bullpen sat the rowdy, irreverent bleacher bums who were more inclined to tan in the summer sun, slug down Narragansett beer, and just raise hell with the right fielder than keep score. On a bad day—of which there were many—they were usually more brutal on the home-team player than the opponent.

I wasn't more than six years old then, oblivious to most everything ex-cept the "Hey, peanuts here!" man, the roar of the crowd, and the rich, green-grassed playing field with its perfect lines, uniform appearance and fine-as-flour dirt—all of which gave the stadium a surreal, cinematic character. It was a storybook world of perfection. The players were big-ger-than-life heroes in the flesh. They lived in the radio, moved through the television, rested under bottle caps, and vacationed in bubble gum cards. I admired them because they transcended normal life and for no other reason than that they were big-league ball players. It was magical to me then.

More than anything, I remember the excitement of seeing the man they called Teddy Ballgame play. He, more than any other athlete, had stirred the emotions and enthusiasm for Boston sports over three decades. He had made Boston the great sports town it was in my childhood and I, like thousands of my generation, reaped the rewards of his presence. This game in 1960 was one of the last he would ever appear in. I had heard that he would retire before the season was over. Ted Williams, the Splen-did Splinter, the Kid, the hero of every boy in New England; the left-handed slugger for whom the right field bullpen was originally designed; the greatest "pure" hitter in baseball, was one of the most feared and loved players throughout pro baseball. One had to feel passionate about him, one way or another. Few players, then or now, have had such an im-pact on kids.

There was one thing about Ted Williams that I could tell even then: he was his own man. Baseball, and hitting in particular, was something at which to excel. It wasn't a game. It wasn't just a job. It wasn't a stepping stone. It certainly wasn't mere entertainment. It was his life, his profession. He was born to hit a baseball. I heard it said that he never tipped his cap. He didn't dialogue with the fans in the left-field grandstand. He didn't have to. He was Ted Williams. His bat did all the saluting and all the hitting a .344 lifetime hitter needed to do. Even as a six-year-old I could feel his pride, a pride many of us seem to lose through the years.

This game in August of 1960 against the East Coast rival Baltimore Orioles was a boy's dream come true. Ted came through as I would always play out in my imaginary games. Ted, my number-one boyhood hero, swatted not one, but two, three-run homers. His three hits single-handedly beat the Orioles 8 to 6. One expected no less than homers from Ted Williams and perhaps that was why people had a love-hate relationship with him; despite a career 521 homers, he disappointed them fourteen out of fifteen times at bat. But I only remembered the homers.

That was the last time I saw Ted Williams as a professional player. After he retired later that season, my father took me to the Indoor Sportsman's Show to watch him fly-cast in an artificial pool with the heavyweight boxer Jack Sharkey. I remember my father hoisting me on his shoulders to snap a photo of Ted with my Kodak Instamatic. I was thrilled to see him and he loved casting for the huge crowd. Yet deep in my heart, knowing what an avid fisherman and professional athlete he was, I always felt a little bit sorry for him to be a spectacle in such a confining environment. For me, it was just a sign that a career and an era were coming to an end.

I visited Fenway Park almost yearly, especially for my birthday in July, even during my college days at Harvard. But I never remembered any game more vividly than that one. After Ted Williams, all the players who followed took a back seat to him and, in many ways, baseball, all sports—all professional sports—and a little bit of me have died. I just didn't know it at the time.

Ted Williams, in his first season with the Bosox, received $3,000. In his heyday, he became the most well-paid ballplayer in the world, commanding $125,000 a year. Yet in his last season, feeling his worth to the club had diminished following a disappointing year, he negotiated his salary *down* by 30 percent. That *never* happens nowadays.

The money ballplayers made back then didn't mean anything to me. Their salaries, whether three thousand or a hundred twenty-five thousand dollars, certainly amounted to a lot of money for me, but I just never thought about it. Real money, money I cared about, was a quarter for a cone from the ice cream man in his white truck lined with colorful pictures of creamsicles, rocket push-ups, and double popsicles. He was always happy to see us come running and screaming from our little brown house to give him a hero's welcome.

"Ding-a-ling, Ice Cream Man!" we'd yell, holding our precious coins, standing on tiptoes, heads barely able to peer into the service window. He didn't appear concerned about making a buck, although I'm sure he did. We didn't know his name, so we called him "Mr. Ice Cream Man," which, I suppose, is not unlike people calling me "Doc." We always said, "Thank you, sir," and he always said, "You're welcome, kids," as he tipped his white cap. It was so simple. Best of all, in the middle of a hot summer, he always had the Red Sox playing on his portable radio. Life couldn't be better.

I don't know if Ted's failure to tip his cap meant he couldn't or wouldn't say "thank you" or "you're welcome." I wasn't even aware at the time that he didn't tip his cap. He claims in his autobiography, *My Turn at Bat,* that sportswriters, his most mortal enemies and yet, unwittingly, his biggest promoters, made a big deal out of that fact but he never gave it much thought. He thought it was a showy part of the game, and he was a purist. A lot of people interpreted that gesture, or the lack of it, as a conscious act of superiority and disregard for the fans, the people who were paying his salary. After all, $125,000 was and, strangely enough to most people, still is a lot of money. Maybe he was doing all he was supposed to and all he wanted to do in this game—hit round-trippers. I certainly never tipped my surgeon's cap after a well-performed operation.

Even though Tom Yawkey, the beloved owner of the Red Sox, was rich—and generous—enough to afford to keep Ted at almost any price, I never thought money was an important issue except, as I later learned in Ted's autobiography, at the very beginning, when he held out for the bonus he thought he deserved and his parents could use. It might have been an issue all along . . . but not like it is today.

It's not that one should begrudge the players their salaries. No one is forcing the owners to pay the exorbitant wages; it's the hallmark of the free-market system, although baseball is not a true free market by any means. Rather, it is a fiercely controlled cartel that has its own internal free-market system. You cannot simply open a major league baseball franchise as you would a corner coffee shop or set out on a career as a professional ballplayer the way a person decides to be a clerk in a department store. To be fair, neither can you easily hang up a shingle and become a doctor—at least not yet. So we have a little in common.

But the fallout from the "money thing" is not that the athlete lives high on the hog for six to eight months of work while the "common man" sweats eight hours a day, twelve months a year. It's not even that they get all the privileges that go along with being sports celebrities, such as being treated as a valuable commodity rather than as a criminal after using illicit drugs, committing rape, or evading taxes, or even that they can get paid millions of dollars for *not* playing on a particular team. While I am not keeping score of athletes versus common men or even baseball players versus plastic surgeons, it does run deeper than the smell of money and the stain of greasy palms. You sense a pride gone flat, a commercialism gone too far, a soul gone wandering. Even the grass, the *artificial* grass, doesn't smell the same. Like it or not, somewhere there is a score between yesterday and today, and today and tomorrow. And I fear I am losing.

■ ■ ■

Baseball. That's what started all this.

The changes that have taken place in baseball since the time I could see myself in my bedroom mirror reflect our environment and shape it as well. Astroturf, domed stadiums, metallic bats, Magnavision, designated hitters . . . and yes, the money.

At the risk of political incorrectness, there have been too many occasions when I felt that the big hand of the public should whack the players—and management—across their collective heads like a parent trying to get a rebellious child to join the rest of the family around the dining room table. Contract disputes created the spring training holdout. Every other year there is talk of a strike. Some years, it actually does happen. Players take precedence over the public. Profits take precedence over boyhood. The individual takes precedence over the team. Loyalty, like family loyalty, is too easily exchanged across both sides of the bargaining table for another decimal point. I never thought it would end up like this.

The Red Sox I knew had players identifiable with the team uniform. Each spring, I could recite the starting lineup which wouldn't change more than a player or two from year to year. Now player loyalty, or management loyalty, extends only as far as the bank account. To me, there was something so comforting and timeless in knowing that Ted Williams was always in left field. The Red Sox versus the Yankees conjured so many deep emotions just like the Celtics versus the Lakers, the Democrats versus the Republicans, capitalism versus communism. Each era represented a generation. Now there are just names of faceless teams, evoking no emotion, certainly little identity, definitely no soul.

It is true that there is more to baseball than just hitting a white ball. The interaction between the game and the public is a symbiotic one. Each feeds off the other. The public needs to feel an affinity for the experience, a personal, everlasting affinity for the sport, like that a youngster had for Ted Williams and the Boston Red Sox.

We have gotten used to the bells and whistles, the brawls, the hype, the cable networks, the expansionism, the sensurround audio systems—each of which, in some way, while trying to make the experience more exciting and accessible, seems to distance the game and the players from the public, their fans. The fact that all these distractions have become necessary speaks for itself.

The money has, in its own way, become the ultimate armor separating the players and the game from the fans. I never had to pay to get Frank Malzone's autograph, even though I might have been willing to do so. It's not that we, as fans or the general public, can't afford the game. Obviously we can. The money being made attests to that.

I used to sit in the grandstand with my father for about $2.75 a seat. We might have been able to afford the boxes, but the grandstand was good enough. That was where the real fans sat. Later, when I was old enough to go with friends without adults chaperoning us, bleacher seats were fine for $1.25. That was where the off-field action was. Profanities offended our ears as much as tobacco smoke assaulted our eyes and noses. Marijuana and beer were the expected fare. But who could argue with the $1.25 seats, especially if you had a chance to catch a home run or even a simple pop foul (which I never ever did)? It was just that possibility, that fantasy, which was exciting.

After paying for the admission ticket, I'd spend another fifty cents on a program to see photos of my favorite players, staring at their faces as though I really knew them, and reading their statistics: earned run averages, runs batted in, batting averages. I read where they were born, where they lived, what their wives' names were. I knew everything about them except their salaries and how much of my $1.25 kept them playing. Money just didn't seem like a big deal at Fenway. It was such a small price for such a big dream.

■ ■ ■

As I remembered those days, I would always spring for the program. But it wasn't for the photos and the stats. It wasn't just for the souvenir. What I really bought the program for was to keep score. That's what it's all about. That's what Grampy taught me.

Grampy was my next-door neighbor's grandfather who taught me how to score the game of baseball. We never called him by his real name, whatever it was. He looked like an old Popeye, smoking his pipe, always cheerful, forever laughing. I recognized the glint in his failing eyes before I saw the wrinkles on his face. Though he was always old to me, he lived to be over ninety, still doing three-point headstands and his own gardening until the day he died. And I never saw him frown or speak in anger.

Grampy would sit with me on the vinyl chairs at the kitchen table. The Westinghouse radio, perched on the formica counter top, volume turned up high, crackled with static and the familiar voices of the Red Sox announcers. We didn't need anything but their voices to bond us with the game.

Grampy would lick his short green pencil, the one with the stubby tip, and with his wooden ruler, draw his own neat scorecard. He'd carefully write in the name of each player in the starting lineup as they were announced and stick an eraser cap on the flat end of the pencil and lick the lead tip once more before the game began. He showed me how to score a strikeout with a K, a bases on balls with a BB, and a groundball double play with a 6-4-3 DP. He would chuckle with pride in his eyes when I correctly scored something difficult: a runner advancing to second on a fielder's choice or a single stretched to a double by an outfielder's error.

During the hot and sticky summer nights, we would sit together into the late evening, listening to the game until the last out was made. The darkness of the night, crickets chirping outside, was a timeless blessing for the two of us.

It didn't seem at all odd at the time—this fat Chinese kid hunched over the scorecard with a weathered old Irish grandfather. Grampy was deaf most of the years I knew him, so I would have to yell right into his ear for him to hear. He never said much, probably because he was so deaf. The cryptic markings on the card was our way of communicating with each other. Through these markings we saw the same fantasy played out in our imagination. We were at the park together. The game became real and tangible. We could almost touch the Green Monster although we never ever saw it in person together. We rarely talked but when he did, Grampy's crisp Irish brogue was music to my ears. What I noticed most of all was that the score always changed. Each game was different. What I realize only now is that I didn't have to see in order to see. Grampy and I, we saw the same things in those scorecards.

Back then, the Red Sox were often the worst team in baseball. The "cellar" had nothing to do with a room in my house but was usually where the Red Sox ended up most seasons. I learned to take those disappointments in stride the way Grampy did through the decades. Winning, losing, the money. It all took a backseat to keeping score.

■   ■   ■

When sitting out in the right field grandstands or bleacher benches, the field felt magically familiar. Lights would signal the balls and strikes on the Green Monster. Green for balls and red for strikes. The number of outs were in yellow. Numbers were manually hung from behind the scoreboard as each run, hit, or error was recorded. There was no large-screen television until years later. No instant replays or fireworks display or mascot cheerleaders. There was a playfully dramatic organ and the unbiased, faceless public announcer. And enough distractions and activities both on the field and in the crowd to keep any little boy occupied.

The Peanuts and Popcorn Man, the Hot Dog Man, the Coke man. The drunken fights, the quarreling Cub Scouts, the colorful beach ball bouncing around the centerfield bleachers. Keeping score tied everything together and centered my attention. Once I lost track of even one play, the whole scorecard was incomplete, like a test with one question left unanswered. How I hated that. It was rare that I left the game to get a snack and rarer still that I left the park before the last out was made.

I doubt if kids today know how to keep score; to keep track of the minutiae in order to get a sense of the big picture; to get behind the fluff and the frills, down to what the game is truly made of. I doubt if many other kids kept score even then. In all probability it was unusual. They were too intent on having fun, perhaps. Today, in Los Angeles, the critics remark about how spoiled the fans are, leaving the game two to three innings early to beat the traffic home. Despite all the trappings to keep the fans interested, one really doesn't have to concentrate on the game too much. There's always instant replay.

Attendance appears to be faltering all over despite population growth. Fans are less enthusiastic except for the really big games. Mass media bring in mega-dollars from advertising and television, so multimillionaires play before acres of empty stadium seats. Expansion and free agency make dynasties short-lived. I have been to a total of three games in the last fifteen years. I haven't watched a complete game on TV as I would have thirty years ago. I certainly haven't listened to even an inning of a game on the radio. With my life running out, I don't have the time. I can't find the interest. People think I'm foolish.

Not long ago, in a fit of nostalgia, I decided to take my parents to a Red Sox game at Fenway Park. This time, *I* drove them to the park. *I* paid for the tickets. *I* bought them Fenway franks with hot mustard. And we sat in the same right-field grandstand, in the green wooden seats destined for the junkyard when they tear Fenway Park down to the historic dirt. The grass looked just as green and the air still smelled of tobacco and marijuana. I couldn't name the starting lineup. But the crowd, including my mother and father, stood up and cheered just as loud when an unknown Red Sox player hit a ball over the Green Monster.

I looked beside me at my parents, both heads graying with wisdom and experience. I realized that I was about the same age my father was when I saw Ted Williams play in 1960. They asked me not to spend so much money on them; after all, the Cokes were now $2.75. I wondered if they knew or cared how much of that $2.75 went to pay for the second baseman's salary. I wondered if they knew I could afford the box seats even though we sat in the grandstand. I wondered where all the time went, how many unmarked scorecards I had passed by, how many games I had missed without my parents sitting in those grandstand seats.

I didn't buy a program because I didn't care about the individual players as I once did when Ted was around. I had already forgotten how to keep score.

Grampy was a great teacher. But now he is dead. As enthusiasm dies so does ability, and vice versa. So it is with me and baseball. I doubt if I could score a single inning correctly. I didn't try that day with my parents. Why bother? Ks and BBs are about all I know now.

I wonder if Grampy would be ashamed of me, having spent all that precious time with me. I don't think so. I'm sure he enjoyed every minute for its own sake just as my parents enjoyed that one game. But it doesn't necessarily make me feel better to think that Grampy would forgive me for not remembering the magic of what he taught me. For now, the best I can do is to close my eyes and smile when I hear the thick Irish brogue and never-ending laughter.

We lost the game, of course. But the time spent with my parents that day wasn't about winning or losing. It wasn't even about keeping score. Perhaps it's only about all those moments we need to keep track of: to have once seen the Green Monster and cheered Ted's homer, to have purchased hot dogs and peanuts for my parents at Fenway Park, and to have kept score with Grampy.

As far as I know, Grampy never kept his scorecard. He just made sure he laughed and yelled during each game. He certainly never worried about players' salaries or the crowd's enthusiasm. He never saw instant replays. But he did love Ted Williams.

If ever I have a grandson I live long enough to watch grow up, or even a next-door neighbor's grandson, he's going to learn how to keep score . . . at least for a while. He'll learn from someone, maybe even from me. He'll learn about Ks and he'll learn about BBs. And perhaps he'll learn that the score always changes.

Always.

2

Friends

"**C**an Dei-Dei come out to play?"
What a wonderful question I used to hear so often when I was growing up. Dei-Dei means 'little brother" in Chinese and everybody in the neighborhood called me by that nickname. It was such a universal thing for kids to do: search out other kids to fool around with. None of us thought anything of it. Today, nobody but my family calls me Dei-Dei and many of us think too much about whom we ask to come out and play.

There were times when I was sick, house-bound, curled up in bed with a thermometer under my tongue. The harsh New England winters would lay claim to my asthmatic lungs or tumescent tonsils. I learned early on how to look into my throat in my bureau mirror, a flashlight searching for those little white dots on my flaming red tonsils. I remember one day when friends came knocking. I watched from the upstairs window as they ran expectantly up the front walk and eagerly asked my mother that familiar question. It was the weekend. I was sick with a cold and those little white dots. There were tons of fresh, white snow on the ground with more falling, a blessing from heaven. It beckoned to me like a soft down comforter.

I loved playing in the snow, building forts, and having snowball fights. The best time was right after it snowed because the snow was clean and sticky. After a night or two of freezing temperatures, the snow, now dirty with grime from the passing cars, would be frozen and unsuitable for making snowballs. We'd have to wait for the weather to warm up and soften it.

I loved snowball fights because they called for a certain amount of controlled aggression—like any sport—and they required individual effort and personal conviction. Though we picked sides, it was your own aim that counted, your tightly packed sphere that whistled through the falling snow. It was your own fearlessness that won the fight.

I always went for the kill and knew how to patiently build a stockpile of hard snowballs so that, when the time came to attack, I could rapid-fire. I would overwhelm my enemy by raining bombs onto his head or cave in his fort with unrelenting firepower and deadly accuracy. I used strategies of finesse, lobbing a soft and easy marshmallow into the enemy's fort, distracting their attention, and, before the shiny decoy fell harmlessly to the ground, fire a blistering round of real ammunition at their exposed and curious heads. It worked every time. I loved bouncing snowballs off my friends' heads.

I was eager to frolic with my friends and they in turn expected me to come out to play. But this time my mother, always erring on the pragmatic side, explained to them that I was sick—yes, *really* sick—and had to stay in. Yes, *had* to! Maybe tomorrow. My heart sank. I felt so sad seeing them leave, waving at them longingly as I resigned myself to spending all day under covers, watching TV, while they rolled around in the wet snow. I took it for granted that I would soon be well and that they'd be back tomorrow. I hated wasting all that perfect snow, and hated being sick. I thought playing was forever and friends would never leave.

Most days, of course, I was perfectly healthy, and if I had finished my homework, household chores, and practicing the violin, I'd run out the door to be with my friends. We'd huddle together, with no particular plans, and the next question would be, "So, what do you want to do?"

"I don't know, Dei Dei. What do you want to do?"

"I don't know. What do *you* want to do?"

This could go back and forth for hours. Eventually we'd have some opinion or make some choice depending on who had been able to come out. There were only a few of us and, while there was always an eldest among us, the decisions seemed equitable. No one friend dominated the group. We only did what we really wanted to do. When we couldn't agree, it didn't seem to matter much and we'd end up doing something any-way—perhaps even quarreling a bit. We knew we'd be back with the same group the next day going over the same questions. The process of the decision, not necessarily the final activity, was the result of our friendship. How we reached our decision was a function of our friendship. No matter what we ultimately ended up playing, we were, first and fore-most, friends, although occasionally, in our disagreement, it would take us a few days to admit that to ourselves.

■ ■ ■

Most of my playful days were spent in the working-class town of Quincy, Massachusetts. There was a park a short walk from my house where we would play on the swings and slides and chase our neighbor's mutt, Pud-dles. In those days a few of us kids could walk to the park together with-out any thought about having an adult with us. As a group, we didn't know what unsafe was. Coming out to the park was a given in life, like having friends.

All towns across America had the same type of park. It wasn't the parks themselves which determined friendships. The park was merely a destination for friends, a place to be with friends. "Dei Dei, let's go to the park." And off we would go. The activities within the park made the park personal and the friendships themselves determined those activities.

In fact, I don't remember the park itself much. The only thing I do re-member is that one summer, a curious story concerning the park circu-lated around the neighborhood. Unlike most slides today, the slides were made of wood rather than aluminum. They were well-used and worn, per-haps even a bit rotted. We heard a rumor that a large splinter had bro-ken off and gone into a girl's butt and up her spinal cord when she slid down too fast. Large to us meant two or three feet long. Being pretty naive, I accepted the rumor as truth, as did all the kids. I doubt that the reality was quite so dramatic (it probably was just that, rumor), but we never used the slide again after that.

Soon, we stopped going to the park altogether. Instead, my friends and I would hike through the wooded area across the street behind some neighbors' houses, where there was a clearing among towering oak trees and dried shrubs. You couldn't call this pit of a place a real park. In fact, we called it "the Pit." The Pit was a favorite playground for our baseball games. The dirt field was filled with stones and small bushes and had no grass whatsoever, just gravel and pebbles.

The "infield" was on an elevated plateau and the "outfield" sloped down twenty feet onto a larger plain that to us seemed to go on for blocks. There was no fence, so a home run really meant that the hitter had to run all the way to home plate—no free trots around the diamond. None of us could ever hit a ball far enough to be completely unplayable, although finding it among the shrubs was often a challenge. Sometimes it would roll under a log or into a deep "pothole." The fact that our baseball turned brown with use didn't make finding it any easier. The rough ground would eventually tear up the seams and eat through the leather so that some of us would literally hit the covers right off the ball and it would unravel on the throw from center to home like a ball of yarn. But we had great times choosing sides by bucking up or tossing the bat and playing our imaginary big league games. Despite all its shortcomings, we never thought of "the Pit" as any less than our private Fenway Park.

Our neighborhood was small and we rarely had enough kids for a full baseball team let alone two sides, so we had to make do with only two infielders or one outfielder or no catcher. We'd choose positions and, even though some had favorite positions, we ended up playing all over the place. We never fought over our choices. We even made up positions like short left center in order to cover three or four positions. It was here that I learned to pitch as well as play first base, shortstop, and outfield all in a single game. Most of all, I learned to play "friends."

We each had our heroes and pretended we were Ted Williams or Whitey Ford or Mickey Mantle. We debated the merits of each and competed with each other in imitating their styles of play. We didn't have a coach or grown-up to teach us the game, so we'd argue about rules and strategies, somehow coming to agreement. I think it was because we liked and respected each other. It didn't matter how right we were, just that we all agreed.

When there were only two of us, we'd play catch in the middle of the street, not worrying about cars in this quiet neighborhood, although I'm sure our parents did. Other times, coming out to play meant shooting marbles or playing with plastic toy soldiers. We'd lie in the driveway shooting colorful marbles, trying to win each other's biggest and most beautiful possession. The ones with the swirls were everyone's favorite.

I loved loading up the smooth, shiny orb, cradling it in the curve of my index finger, cocking my thumb against the inside part of the middle finger and letting it fly as hard as I could. It was exhilarating to watch the marbles scatter all over the driveway from a direct hit. We practiced combination and ricochet shots. No matter how many marbles any of us won, we never seemed to run out. To us, the marbles were a measure of our friendship. We hated it when we lost a favorite one and argued when someone ended up with too many, but we always made sure each of us had some marbles so that none of us was left with an empty box. What good was it if one person ended up with all the marbles?

Our toy soldiers ended up in the sandbox at the bottom of our backyard, hiding in foxholes or trenches, or marching across vast desert dunes. Why we found playing with inanimate toy soldiers fun, I really don't know. They didn't have moving parts or colorful uniforms. They all looked the same. We had to work to bring them alive. By the time we got our imaginations going to simulate real situations and actual actions in these masses of plastic, we were mesmerized. Our imagination deepened and somehow we were hooked. Suddenly we had a whole army of friends.

Having playmates think the same way encouraged the play. We had to be on the same wavelength to make it worthwhile. It made no sense if my men were running up a mountain to attack a fort if my friend, the enemy, was marching his men across an unrelated barren desert. Playing make-believe is a form of mutual hypnosis. The danger is thinking that what happens in fantasy can carry over into reality.

Friends had to understand that just because you wiped out a whole battalion of foot soldiers, you need not get personally upset at your best friend. Somehow, we understood that. I don't remember ever wanting to kill my neighbor for beating up my toy soldiers.

When one of us would get bored with playing make-believe, we'd sacrifice our toy soldiers for real. We'd tie a soldier to a branch and set it afire like a marshmallow. The plastic man melted into a zip gun, making a sizzling, zipping noise as the red-hot plastic droplets zapped other soldiers lying helplessly in the sandbox. It was grotesque but we did it more for the zip than for the zap. That was infinitely more fun than just pretending that bombs were destroying a friend's army. Contrary to what is touted by child psychologists and educators today, none of us turned into a sadist or war-mongerer.

When I was alone at home, I never lacked for something to do. Everything was interesting to me. With so many activities, I never felt lonely. Having friends drop over unannounced didn't surprise me. It was expected. And even when I didn't feel like doing anything special, I liked having them ask. The feeling was undoubtedly mutual; the desire for friendship is a common bond all kids have. Being alone is okay, but having friends is better.

While my mother and father set guidelines—don't interrupt a neighbor during dinner and don't stay out too late—I didn't feel at all self-conscious about looking for playmates. Like many kids, there were times when I wanted to go play with friends before dinner was over. In fact, I *had* to go visit. I'd inhale my meatloaf and run next door. Friends play such an unassuming and important role in our early lives. They are more important than eating; at times more important than even parents. Certainly more important than big sisters, at least when you're little.

When we moved to Newton, a wealthier, middle- to upper-middle-class community outside of Boston, friends revolved around school and less around the neighborhood. My family moved to Newton because of the outstanding school system which ranked in the country's top ten during the 1960s. Little thought was given to whether we'd fit into the neighborhood or who the neighbors were. It turned out that we lived in our Newton house for years without socializing with our next-door neighbors, but not because we didn't get along with them. Our priorities were elsewhere and it also seemed as if no new neighborhood could ever replace the one we left behind. This situation is not uncommon.

School was more important than socializing. No telling where I would be today if my parents had not the foresight to put educational opportunities first on their priority list.

However, despite the superlative education, I barely knew the neighbors' kids. Those I did know, I knew because I went to school with them. Rarely did classmates live right next door to each other. Events were generally planned around group or school activities: Saturday morning youth orchestra rehearsal, Saturday night bridge, Wednesday evening musical soirées, Thursday afternoon football practice, Sunday morning matzohbrei when we would whip up a huge batch of the Jewish version of French toast dripping with maple syrup. Occasionally there were impromptu touch football games in the street or Chinese fire drills on Heartbreak Hill (the hill made famous for knocking more than a few runners out of the Boston Marathon because of its unrelenting uphill gradient twenty miles into the race).

School activities bonded many friendships: the teams, the clubs, the Honor Society, the musical groups. Each had its score of potential friends and playmates. Getting together after school was a regular habit. All it generally required was a phone call. Yet, since friends from school lived farther away than the immediate neighborhood and few of us drove, dropping in at one's house unannounced became an infrequent event. And since my life, like most kids' lives, was compartmentalized into these groups, so were my friends. Who I did things with was determined not by proximity but by activities. Friends were selected in or out by activities rather than the other way around. If you didn't play football, you didn't hang out with the football crowd. If you didn't play music, you didn't become friends with musicians. That's how cliques form.

I never realized this at the time. Few did. My high school graduating class had over eight hundred students, so it wasn't a problem making friends with somebody. There were certainly enough pretty girls and plenty of kids with common interests. Selecting friends was a natural, if not an all-too-conscious, process. We didn't have to accept friends if we didn't want to. Perhaps I wasn't as aware of the fact that sometimes they didn't want to accept me either. Natural selection goes both ways.

■　■　■

College poses a dual problem. Dorms create pseudo-neighborhoods where students live, study, and even fight with each other while classes and activities present opportunities for building long-lasting friendships. Yet all activities compete with each other to influence our friendships. There can be too many obligations and too many opportunities; too much pressure and too much ambition; too much on the mind to really enjoy friends. While walking through Harvard Yard in the evening during final exam time, I could feel the agitated brainwaves of students cramming, electrifying the darkness, piercing the ignorance of the world. We would help each other, but in the end, it was all about us as individuals. I expected the universe to explode with all the self-driven competition.

Friends became secondary to the activities and the self. Harvard was a place to find what one was really made of. It was a place where Dei Dei grew up. You see, everybody at Harvard is a somebody who can quickly become a nobody. No matter how good you were at anything, there always seemed to be someone better at Harvard. Imagine being a well-decorated valedictorian in high school (I was runner-up runner-up valedictorian, but I *can* imagine) and then finding yourself in a sea of valedictorians. You had to find that one thing that made you special. Some people never find it because you can't find it only in friends. Others don't find it because they don't realize that all they may need is a friend. A balance to life is the key.

One of my friends in the freshman class was a fifteen-year-old Chinese girl from Canada, obviously brilliant, but deathly shy. I respected, even somewhat envied, her because she was a year younger than me and I proudly thought that I was pretty young to be a graduate from Harvard at nineteen. She didn't say much, even at parties. She was thin and fair-skinned, very frail-looking, even sickly. Everything in class appeared easy for her, especially the sciences. She was a bonafide whiz kid. She had everything to look forward to at Harvard—until she threw herself off a three-story dorm in the freezing midnight cold of a violent New England nor'easter. Perhaps she only needed a friend but couldn't find one among Chaucer's tales, Fermi's theorem, or Kreb's cycle. I survived knowing I was the youngest, best-looking, and smartest tennis-playing Chinese violinist who ever swung a squash racquet at Harvard. That and a few good friends got me through.

One good thing was, you couldn't fail Harvard. Once you were in, you were in. There were only two proscriptions: don't plagiarize and do return all your library books. Big dreams, big rewards awaited the diligent and studious. Most students had their sights set on bigger things than playmates. And that included me.

This only intensified in medical school where friends were even more single-minded and the stakes for some even higher. Nothing feels like the old neighborhood. Growing older and more mature, we can exercise choice, so I chose to withdrew from dorm life in medical school to live in my own converted condominium on the Fens, a stone's throw from my beloved Fenway Park. Once I became old enough and independent enough to reject friendships based solely on neighborhoods or founded in organizational groups, it became easier to be selective. One learns life as an individual.

■ ■ ■

With school done, the job becomes the focal point. The ties are mainly professional. Playmates disappear. Classmates scatter throughout the country. Neighbors are insular. The phone is quiet save for the family, love interest, or job concern. Friends are busy and phone calls frequently end up with one answering machine talking to another answering machine. Friends can truly come from anywhere. Or one can select oneself into isolation.

Planned events are productions, coordinating multiple, independent schedules and various conflicting obligations. Most evenings are spent alone: reading, writing, thinking, brooding. Mostly brooding. Neighbors don't knock anymore. I've met only one. I'm sure I'm not alone in that respect.

I find myself becoming afraid that I'll never again hear anyone ask, "Can Dei-Dei come out to play?" That fear is not unfounded. I expect that no one will knock on my door unannounced and that I won't be phoned by a friend who just wants to drop by without a real reason. I can't imagine three middle-aged men sitting on a driveway asking each other, "What do you want to do?" "I don't know. What do *you* want to do?" Many of my female friends have left singlehood and have new babies. Those who haven't, have no reason to call. Anyway, my wife, Joanne, wouldn't let them.

We have all become insular and thus are guilty and in danger of losing the neighborhood of adolescence. I fear asking friends to come out to "play." They have their own lives, their own playmates, their own classmates. Spouses and children hold them captive. I also fear rejection, of being told no, they are not "sick" or not "at home." They simply "can't" or "don't want to come out to play." There are more important matters.

I don't think it is depression or a result of realizing my life is half over. It's not self-pity or longing. It's a fact. Our world is much larger than the old neighborhood of four or five houses. Parks are still parks, albeit a lot less safe, but friends—true friends you wouldn't hesitate to bombard with cold, hard snowballs or trade toy soldier stories with—are scarce. They are neither just next door nor merely a phone call away. We communicate once a year, twice a decade. Most are truly in another world.

Soon, those people who are more than half dead might not even be able to hear the phone ring. Even if it did, and they could still hear, they might not remember their friends. In the end, it might be all they live for.

I have a nagging thought that all the friendships we build in life, particularly in childhood, are for naught if life itself does not exist in them. It is as if the pain and terror of a horrible accident does not have meaning if the brain is smashed to a senseless pulp; the joys of a dream are left unappreciated, hanging in space, if we cannot wake from the sleep and, just as quickly, jump back into that dream. Those many snowballs that we rained on our favorite playmates are as an illusion or fantasy, as much as the toy soldiers marching across the desert dunes, unless we can, later in life, laugh with that playmate about our many battles years ago.

There will be those who read this and instinctively mutter, "Get a life!"

I have a life. It is a full one. Where I live in southern California, the weather is terrific. Activities are endless. Work is generally fulfilling. People are pleasant. The beaches are close by. The desert is close by. The mountains are close by. There is even snow on those mountains in winter.

But for all those wonderful things, I lament that I will never again mash a handful of moist, fresh snow into a hardened missile of boyhood joy. And even if I did, I wouldn't know who to launch it at—certainly not the neighbor across the street. I might even relish the thought of being hit myself.

Today, I get into my convertible to drop off some legal paperwork at my attorney's house. The sun is shining and the ocean breeze whips at my hair. The roads are packed with traffic. Everyone is going somewhere. Some alone. Others seem surrounded by friends. The radio livens the air with music, all kinds of music.

I am alone today. I wonder whom I can visit.

It is a simple thought. One without an answer, without a reason. I feel a snowball whistle by my ear. It's just a thought. Perhaps it's only the wind.

On my way back home, knowing a friend, his wife, and kids (whose names I've already forgotten) are just blocks away, I brave the self-consciousness and the fear of intrusion. I drive directly to his home. Full of a love for life, I park the car and bound determinedly up the front walkway. I think to myself, "I will not be conquered by age. I will not be defeated by the passing of time. I will not relinquish that which is so vital to human existence. I will not succumb to a life of only memories and more memories."

I hesitate ever so slightly at the front door. Doubt creeps in. He was never my classmate. He isn't my neighbor. I don't know his hobbies. We work together infrequently. He has a wife and two kids. Perhaps he's busy. Maybe he's not at home. What if he's sick? I never thought so much as a kid.

None of this really matters. I don't have anything to talk about specifically and so what if he's not at home. I'm not doing this for him.

I reach for the buzzer and press firmly. I wait childishly. I have no plans, no marbles, no toy soldiers. I ring again.

"Hello?"

I let out a sigh. Finally.

"It's Robin."

I wait. A lifetime. I wish I were in a park.

The door flies opens.

3

Eggs

I had my first sexual encounter around age five. I remember lying in my tiny bed, covered with my brown, woolly cowboy blanket, mesmerized by my baby sitter's body silhouetted against the hallway light. She entered the room and disappeared into the darkness around me. Her invisible hands drew the covers protectively about my body high up under my chin and, out of the black nothingness, she kissed me good night on the cheeks. Being such a good and obedient kid, I never gave her any trouble, never vomited on her, never tied her to a chair. I figured I earned that kiss.

From that kiss I would drift off into an innocent sleep. What my baby sitter did after that, I never knew. She couldn't have been more than fourteen or fifteen. The nights passed quickly and peacefully, and I wouldn't awaken until breakfast—to the smell of my mom's bacon and eggs. I'm sure I had sexual fantasies during childhood although most of them are long forgotten.

Friends at a boy's summer camp during my teen years once told me that I was sexually aroused during a beach party held with the girl's camp across the lake. I was probably around twelve and wasn't even sure what they meant. I didn't feel anything special and never thought to look in my bathing trunks. I assumed they were just putting me on since they were older, presumably wiser, and definitely more mischievous. I liked girls, even admired them. They fascinated me because they were so different from boys: so beautiful to look at and so gentle. But I truly doubt I was sexually aroused by them at such an early age. That was too foreign to me. The closest thing to pornography or sexually stimulating material to me at that age was Veronica and Betty in the Archie comics. I don't think I even reached puberty until sometime in college.

If I was immature at anything, I guess sexuality was it. I never kissed anyone in junior high and that probably constitutes being stunted by today's standards. My first real face-sucker was in high school with J. We were at a party in a friend's home. The parents were out. I wasn't even dating her at the time. But, kids being kids, we somehow ended up rolling on the carpet between twin beds in the guest room. It was pretty dark (most sexual experiences take place in the dark—literally and figuratively). Anyway, J. was quite surprised by the kiss. Not because she didn't expect it (she was the one who pulled *me* to the ground), but because somehow my tongue ended up in her mouth.

"Where did you learn to kiss like *that*?" she asked breathlessly. I thought she sounded incredulous, but it might have been that I was lying on her very mature chest.

I was taken aback. At first I thought I had done something wrong. But then, realizing she actually enjoyed it, I was surprised that she was surprised because I thought everyone kissed like that. It felt very natural to me. No one coached me. I didn't hang out in boy's rooms. There weren't any smooching manuals that I knew of. I didn't think anything of it.

Thanks to J., I've made love all these years thinking that I was someone special because what came natural to me seemed so extraordinary to others. I don't mean that in a perverted or egotistical way, but just as a self-reassuring thought. Everyone should be so fortunate!

Of course they *all* said how special and sensitive and different I was. I never really knew for sure. You never really know what women think. Is it just a feminine ploy to condition and train men or cater to their penile egos? That possibility—even probability—was always unsettling to me, especially as I grew older and gained insight into male-female interaction, realizing what they were capable of. Being the egotistical person I am, I chose to assume that I was truly extraordinary. I figured you've got to start *somewhere*!

I didn't go on a real date until my senior year in high school and a true sexual experience came only in college, when I finally got broken in. I had at least two solid girlfriends during this time, great women whom I dated for two to three years each. In and around these "serious" relationships, I had a few other encounters—most quite memorable, some rather forgettable. I don't mean forgettable in that they didn't mean anything to me at the time. They did and they should. (Any time two human beings strip away enough of themselves to allow each into the other's life in a way mothers and fathers, sister and brothers can't, should be meaningful.) By forgettable I mean that forgetting them didn't cause pain in the long run. I could forget (and obviously so could they) without feeling sad or lonely or angry or guilty.

It's important to be able to have forgettable sex (not necessarily meaningless sex), otherwise we'd all be crushed by the weight of it all. Mutually forgettable sex usually doesn't end up in murder or mental depression. Hopefully. It is a wonderfully positive, ego-building, mutually respectful experience. But it is not life or death.

If you were to plot out the frequency of my lovemaking over the years, I think it would be rather consistent, with maybe a big blip—okay, a little blip—around a decade or so ago, during the hedonistic 1980s when I still had lots of hair on top. Most people experience that blip; think about when it happened to you. But if you were to plot out the number of different partners I've had over time, it would take a dramatic plunge after the blip.

Now, any man worth his weight in manhood would cringe at the thought of declining sexuality as the years go by. I am no exception. I know I passed my sexual prime many years ago. That's what the book says about us males physiologically. Unfortunately, I wasn't prepared to take advantage of that knowledge. Most men aren't. Social norms often don't coincide with scientific reality. Here, age creeps up and taunts us with ex-post-facto truths. Like picking stocks, we realize what we could have done much too late. We weren't like boys are nowadays.

My little blip occurred without my even knowing it was a blip and with such restraint that had I known it wouldn't last, I'd have savored each moment a little more. Those days are gone.

■   ■   ■

Over the years, I've realized that there are basically two types of sexual interaction. In one you make love and leave; in the other you make love and hang around. I guess one is more "just sex" and the other is more "making love," although where and how you cross from one to the other is not all that clear. It's a point at which meaningless turns into forgettable and forgettable somehow becomes memorable. In general, the clue lies in what happens after the physical act. It's not the foreplay or the play itself that's important. It's the afterplay.

Since many of those years were spent without a steady girlfriend, sexual relationships were often relatively brief. I don't mean a few minutes or hours brief—I don't remember ever picking up a girl just to go to bed with her—but usually a few weeks or months brief.

Back in those coveted days of the 1980s I viewed sex as an extension of friendship—a humanistic, not animalistic, instinct. I thought, it is the reward I get or the gift I give for being a woman's friend. I didn't see much value in sharing a bed with someone you didn't care about unless you just needed to catch a little shuteye. Most of my lovemaking was with people I considered friends but was not necessarily committed to as if in a full-fledged relationship. It wasn't by design. It simply happened that way. Besides the rather obvious physical attraction, the minimum lovers need is mutual empathy. Friends are great for that—not all friends, just some of them. I can't think of anyone I'd more like to spend an intimate moment with than a *really* good friend.

Like many sexual encounters in America, Europe, or across Asia, the lovemaking often ends with the man zipping up his pants, trekking across the room, and slipping out the door. Occasionally it would result in a deep slumber . . . from which the man would arise, trek across the room, and proceed to slip out the door. I was no different and being a doctor tied to his beeper for the last fifteen years, it wasn't always by choice.

While lovemaking was usually great, the time out the door varied tremendously. Though I rarely made love to a girl just once, the trek to the door was consistent. I think the women I was with at these times understood this. In fact, it wasn't uncommon for them to do the trekking. It's always a two-way forgettable path to that door. And women's lib was in full swing by then!

I suppose that early on in my halcyon days, the time to the door was relatively short. I did talk after lovemaking, albeit in disjointed, slurred half-sentences. Sometimes my partner and I did stupid things like watch foreign movies on TV or eat stale leftovers. Most of the time, we would sink restfully into bed and after a few moments of quiet meditation, one of us would start trekking. I don't remember ever taking time to scramble eggs.

It is true that all this can make one feel emotionally empty. I suppose my partners felt the same. I didn't take a poll. It's usually a sign that forgettable sex is getting dangerously close to being meaningless or memorable. I learned to control the part of me that craved passion. Wanting passion and feeling it can be mutually exclusive. You can want to be passionate with someone and never feel it. Likewise, you can feel passion without really wanting it. I accept that that is part of being human. I do know for a fact that some of the emotional drain is purely hormonal and physiological. Passion leaves the body by way of sex secretions. No wonder castration is so effective in diminishing sex drive.

There were times when I wanted to leave much sooner, but stayed out of politeness. (I can hear the collective groan.) Yet, there were other times when I wanted to stay longer, but knew it was best not to. So the time between lovemaking and leaving averaged . . . oh, about thirty-eight minutes. While there was a large variation, luckily, most of those friendships lasted much longer.

My most memorable and meaningful sexual encounters were usually with my closest women friends—not that I slept with all my close female friends but the more I knew a person, the more we were "friends," the longer it took to sleep together. And the longer it took to sleep together, the more it meant to us, and thus the longer it took for one of us to start trekking. Part of it, I suppose, was that both of us were usually paralyzed with embarrassment. It kept us from bolting for the door. It's amazing how quickly grunts deteriorate to giggles. Actually, it's a very nice feeling being with a friend, sort of like having covers drawn around your body.

However, what I'm concerned about is not sexuality, but the loss of it. It's no secret that sexual identity is an important part of a person's self. In fact, the presence or absence of sexual identity may be the most important determinant of social behavior. Much of what men and women do is related to sexuality in its broadest sense. The job we hold has varying degrees of attraction to the opposite sex, as do the cars we drive, the clothes we wear, and the colognes or perfumes and makeup we use. How we act is often a reflection of our sexual confidence or sexual inadequacy. It may determine how we treat one another. Certainly, entering that part of life called marriage has everything to do with sexual attraction on more than just a physical level.

■　■　■

Some interesting encounters following my baby sitter and J. helped make me more aware of my sexual identity, which in turn makes me fear losing it more and more as each day goes on. I was always quite timid, so that every victory won was a blessing. To surrender now seems unbearably premature and defeatist.

There was a statuesque nurse who used to work in one of the training hospitals during my surgical training. She must have been close to six feet tall with silky blond hair, a slender, shapely body and a very sensuous swing to her walk. It wasn't in an overtly lascivious way, but just natural and gentle. Her skin was incredibly light, soft, and translucent and she spoke in a melodious feminine whisper, her tone rising and falling with each movement of her perfect breasts. She would sometimes turn her head so that she gazed at me ever so coyly from the corners of her almond eyes. It was no wonder that I was attracted to her as was practically the entire male hospital staff. However, beneath the sexuality, there was something more curious, as if she were half hiding behind it and half afraid of it.

We had a great time working together, joking around, teasing each other with our veiled innuendos. Today, she might have cried sexual harassment, although she was the one who usually started it!

We were comfortably Platonic with each other, even if the sexual tension fired up the hospital hallways like electro-cardioversion. She finally invited me to her apartment one weekend to do what most nurses did for resident doctors—that's right, feed them! Dinner was undoubtedly delicious (whatever it was had to be better than hospital food). We felt close and relaxed, but not especially romantic. Then we ended up in the apartment complex jacuzzi, the single most common prop for sexual foreplay in the eighties. One thing led to another and we soon were kissing.

She was very sensual and I'd be lying if I didn't say I was aroused. By then, having taken quite a few anatomy, biology, and human sexuality courses, I knew what sexual arousal meant. Even so, I could sense a hesitancy on her part that went beyond just the sex thing. Don't ask me how I knew. I just did. I could sense a vulnerability that wasn't purely embarrassment. She wasn't giggling and I wasn't sexually aggressive or desperate, just searching for that elusive empathy. She drew back.

"I need to tell you something."

"What?"

"My parents raised me as a boy."

"So? What's wrong with being a tomboy?" I thought. It was hard to assume a completely clinical stance while half-naked in the jacuzzi, listening to her as an understanding physician would his patient.

"I never felt like a boy." She was dead serious now.

"So?" I thought again.

Then it hit me. She had been brought up as a boy, because she *was* a boy! She had undergone a sex change operation as a teenager; hormones and plastic surgery had made her the statuesque beauty she was.

Now one stereotypical reaction as a self-professed heterosexual would have been for me to dash for the nearest water source (besides the jacuzzi water into which we were sweating), wash my mouth out with bleach, and run gagging out the door fast. The other stereotypical reaction as a budding clinician would have been for me to check out her scars. But I did neither. I sensed how difficult it was for her to do what she did, not only to allow me to get close enough physically, but to reveal such a deep and private secret to me, a secret so unsuspected and bizarre. Everyone thought she was a knockout woman. I'm sure she was aware of that, even desired it. The thing that transsexuals want the most is to be accepted and treated like the gender they feel they are. I suspect that even though she felt she might have gotten away with it (let's face it, plenty of the women in L.A. are rebuilt in one way or another), sooner or later she would have had to tell the man she chose to be with and eventually suffer the consequences of his reaction.

It was a no-win situation for her.

As for me, as much as I was physically aroused, I was already satisfied that she found me sexually and humanly attractive enough to be in the impossible position we were in.

We never made love. I know it sounds hypocritical to say it just didn't feel right. I know I took my time to trek out the door that evening. But letting me in on her secret was more emotional to both of us than any physical sex. We had found that elusive empathy. That was enough. You can't stay in a jacuzzi in 104-degree water forever. We both knew the water was just too hot. It is justice that we must strip ourselves naked in order to make love. And once our emotions and souls are bared, the physicalness becomes secondary. Though still friends, we never went out again after that. She soon left the hospital and I never heard from her again. No-win. I still sweat whenever I think of that night.

A year earlier, I had a massive crush on another nurse in a different hospital. Why are they always nurses? She was a fun-loving, kind person who seemed in control of everything, at work or at play. She wasn't someone who embarrassed easily.

The first time she consented to go out with me (and it took some polite urging), we ended up talking about her menstrual cycle. Although she, too, was from back East, I thought it was so L.A.-ish to be calmly discussing something so intimate and personal with someone I didn't even know. (At that time, L.A. was known to be *so* friendly.) I guess that's how one gets to know someone. The incongruity of the moment was even more startling because the date took place in a bustling, noisy restaurant with dozens of strangers eavesdropping. Having gotten through such a revealing conversation that evening, it is no wonder I became enamored of her. Being tall, brunette, and curvaceous didn't hurt either.

Unfortunately for me, she was in the throes of an on-again-off-again relationship with another resident from out of state. So we became good friends instead: talking, hiking, biking, going to movies together. We had a true companionship without commitment.

Then there came a time when she was in one of the many off-again hiatuses with her boyfriend and I had broken up with my girlfriend. She invited me over for—what else?—dinner. We had some wine. She could drink. I couldn't handle it. We started to feel that thing. You know. Empathy.

Soon she—yes, *she*—was leading me onto her bed, a simple mattress lying on the carpeted floor. She began to kiss voraciously without saying a word, as if I were dessert. It was the very first time I felt she had any desire for me sexually. And she wasn't at all afraid to let it be known.

It was at that moment in time that I learned two things. One, a mature woman can be just as sexually needy and aggressive as a man (this "woman-as-victim" or "woman-as-timid-kitten" is a lie, another feminine ploy perhaps). And two, wine and sex don't mix for me. My mind said "Yessiree!" but my body asked "How?" You can't imagine how small that made me feel, in more ways than one.

Once again, I never made love to her. I blamed it on the cabernet. Maybe it was her sexual aggressiveness which caught me off-guard. Or perhaps it was the fact that, by now, I knew her boyfriend. We ended up just cuddling, talking about our feelings, her relationship, my body's reaction to alcohol. "It's the alcohol. It's the alcohol!" I apologized all night long. She didn't seem upset. She laughed.

I finally went trekking later that evening. We never dated again after that. She soon settled down with her boyfriend whom she eventually married. My girlfriend also got married a couple of years later. One good thing about being with me back then: most women who left me married the next guy they were with. This was yet another in a series of unforgettably forgettable non-sex encounters which has left me with so much food for thought, and a longing for the memorable sex.

■　　■　　■

As I age, I fear the loss of physical attraction, the diminishing of my sexuality in all respects, the lack of newly enriching encounters such as these. I suppose it's only natural. With the specter of deadly sexually transmitted diseases and the return of more traditional values, the days of frequent trekking are gone.

I go back to when I was dating the woman who was to become my wife, when we were just planning marriage. Or, as I tremblingly put it, m, m, m . . . marriage. We had been together for seven plus years. She likes to count from the day we first met and emotions started afluttering. I, like most guys, like to count from the latest day possible, the day she returned to me after permanently leaving her last boyfriend. There is a contested period of at least seven months. It doesn't really matter. It's still a long time.

We both had twinges then of the seven-year itch; it often makes us want to scratch the skin off our bones. We'd been through best friends' weddings, parental divorces, and our own multitude of separations and reconciliations. We'd laughed until we'd wheezed and cried ourselves dry. There are sexually voracious times and sexually famished times. We have missed each other painfully. And we have wished each other dead and minced into tiny, bite-sized pieces.

We make love now like so many married couples—less frequently than when we were dating and with too much familiarity. Rather than being spontaneous, we find ourselves debating the pros and cons of making love to each other at some negotiated future point in time. The real saving grace is that both of us love to eat.

Sometimes we'd rather eat than make love. Other times, we'd make love and then eat. In the seven or eight years we've known each other, neither of us has gone trekking, at least not after making love and before eating. There is something so secure about not having to worry about how and when to leave after lovemaking, and just worrying about what one is going to eat. I've certainly spent more post-lovemaking time with her than anyone else.

Sunday mornings are our favorite time. Even though we arise at different hours—I usually get up around seven while she luxuriates in bed until noon—Sunday is the day we try to have brunch together. We both love eggs, although with our recent concern for fat and cholesterol intake we are more apt to scramble nonfat, noncholesterol imitation eggs. On some days we give in and use the real thing. Whatever the egg, a great day for us is eating eggs after making love. So wholesome.

This time, trekking occurs together, hand in hand, toward the refrigerator door or our local coffee shop or deli for an omelette or plate of scrambled eggs, lox, and onions. We love that time, feeding our faces after satisfying our passions. We can look each other in the eye and talk about menstrual cycles, transsexualism, or nothing at all. We can scramble, poach, fry, boil our eggs. It doesn't matter, neither of us is going anyplace.

I'm still afraid of the trend on the graph: afraid of growing old, feeling old, acting old, losing out. I can only fantasize about extraordinary sexual encounters and hope other women think fondly of me. But one thing I now know and can say with some insight, without worry, without regret, without guilt: "Things just seem to get better with eggs."

4

Fat, Food, and Fast Food

I see two fat wedges of dark, creamy chocolate cake sitting seductively before two fat wads of human flesh at the next table. The sweet smell of cocoa is so thick I lick at the air for a taste. I remember the Schrafft's chocolate factory back in my cherubic youth, spewing the simple pleasures of childhood out its steaming ventilation stacks. Other luscious choices go by on a tray before me and I subconsciously rub my belly to feel the roll of fat, giving me the strength to say, "No, thanks." It is a reminder of what was, is, and will be.

I'm not really a sweet-tooth type of person. In fact, I don't like chocolate much. But it does smell great. At this stage in life, I rarely indulge in rich desserts; yet it's as if I'm still denying myself even if I admit I don't want it in the first place. Guilt by association.

Denial wasn't always the case. We all remember the days of Twinkies, Ding Dongs, Chunkies, and Crackerjacks. I had them all. We were all sucked in by effective and addictive commercials. Those were the formative years of junk food junkies. Nutritional education amounted to three square meals a day and who knows what in between, and the FDA didn't care what got wrapped, bottled, or packaged. Candy companies had the kids' whole world at their collective feet. I don't think there have been any truly revolutionary strides in candy products since then.

Besides candy, there was plenty of ice cream. *Real* ice cream with *real* cream and *real* sugar. We didn't know about yogurt or saccharin or fat-free ice cream yet. Then there were strawberry shortcakes (homemade with moist pound cake, frozen strawberries in syrup and a topping of whipped cream), fruit cocktail with hideously red cherries swimming in fructose, pudding mixes, angel food cake, and, of course, fluffernutter marshmallow sandwiches. The list goes on and on.

Whether in school, at home, or with friends, I didn't give eating much thought. It was just the thing to do. Like breathing, it was constant, nonstop, with the occasional excessive inhalation.

■ ■ ■

I was born weighing eight pounds, seven ounces—not particularly over-sized. But that was the last time weight *wasn't* an issue. Three months before I turned three, I was in the 99th percentile for weight at over forty pounds and by the time I was twelve, I weighed one hundred sixty. I finally topped out at one hundred eighty-something at sixteen. I won't mention how much I weigh now, but it ain't less than one eighty.

I always liked food. I enjoyed the act of eating. Such a pleasurable array of sensations: from the aroma filling my head, to the stimulated taste buds and tingling in my tongue, to the sensuous bolus sliding down the esophagus. Food went into my mouth with little thought or honest appreciation. It was a reflex thing, like sexual arousal used to be. Back then, we didn't obsess or count calories. Like sex during the sexual revolution, we just did it. Babies sucking on thumbs.

I'm sure I was conditioned to some extent at home: those "millions of poor starving people in China." It was a cliché, but in our family it carried extra weight. After all, who, if not my parents—both relatively fresh-off-the-boat immigrants from the mainland in the late 1940s—should know? That statement alone was usually enough to get me to eat everything in sight, as if my guilt-ridden splurge would spare those poor starving Chinese their hunger pangs. It seemed futile and irrational. You'd think that we should have actually eaten *less* and sent leftovers to China!

Naturally, that wasn't the case, so I ended up saving the whole city of Shanghai many times over during my childhood. Every plateful represented one family of four. I became so indoctrinated that I couldn't stand to see food wasted. I quickly developed a behavior justifying my nickname at home—the human garbage disposal. Everything digestible went into my mouth. When we ate at home I cleaned off everyone's plate. When we went out I never refused dessert. And when we left the restaurant, if I didn't finish every last edible morsel, you could bet I was stuffed to my eyeballs and carrying a doggie bag.

My mother loves to tell the story of how, as a roly-poly ball of fat, I ate and ate and ate until I threw up all over her friends. It must have been pretty cute at the time because she tells it to everyone. It was one of the first tales she told my wife when we were first dating. Obviously it made an indelible, if not delectable, impression.

I can see my mother with her Chinese friends—my "aunties"— laughing about my eating habits as they scolded me. Each had her own son—some bigger, some smaller than me.

"Eat. Grow up strong."

"Don't eat. You're too fat."

"Eat. Your mother's cooking so good."

"Don't eat. Not healthy to eat so much."

"Eat. I cook plenty of food."

"Don't need to eat. My cooking not too good."

The millions of poor starving people in China . . .

As I grew older, I had more self-control and learned to stop at a point just before I had to vomit. I don't think anyone really thought this type of behavior was a disease. Today, every and any behavior is. It wasn't like bulimia or anything. It was mainly physiological: I just loved the taste of food.

But I'm sure there is something psychological behind it: a prolonged, intense oral phase of development, or an outlet for pleasurable sensations, perhaps a craving for attention. Infants are like parasites sucking up all the nutrients with which we indulge them. There's nothing more satisfying than seeing a chubby baby voraciously sucking on a bottle.

"Good baby. Eat and make Mommy happy."

Eating and food are so basic to human survival, they are used consciously or subconsciously as expressions of emotions. How many kids have experienced the anger of a parent by going to bed hungry? How many have been praised for finishing every morsel on their plate? Each is pretty unambiguous. I know. I've been there.

There are millions of others who have what is now commonly referred to as an *eating disorder*. American men and women are forever dieting, for one reason or another. My sister went through a phase of development, or maybe it was regression, when eating disorders were commonplace. She took dieting and looking thin to such an extreme that her menstrual cycle stopped for months. That's one way your body tells you you're going a bit too far—like involuntary vomiting. Of course, one person's eating disorder is another person's cure.

As a surgical resident, I had patients with Willi-Prader syndrome: huge, morbidly obese kids with insatiable appetites. Their brains don't know how or when to turn off the hunger signal. They don't know how to feel full or when to stop. Their fat just grows and grows, engulfing their whole life. A touch of anorexia would be a blessing.

So it is. First fat is cute. Then it's a disease. Later it's just disgusting.

I'm hanging around the disgusting phase, which is sometimes a good definition for the middle-age physique. Not that I'm morbidly obese or anything. I'm not. I'm just not cute or diseased. I do have extra fat in some spots that, while quite common for males my age, is still quite disgusting to me. They say obesity starts early in life and carries through adulthood. Once a fat kid, always a fat adult. That's not entirely true, but a good excuse if I was looking for one. The only good thing about the extra fat is that it can become a great deterrent to overeating. I just grab a handful of flab around my waist and my appetite for fat-storing culinary delights quickly subsides. The harder I squeeze, the less inclined I am to gorge.

So it wasn't all that hard giving up the slice of chocolate cake at the next table. After all, it would be extremely hard for me to eat with both hands glued to my midsection, trying to convince myself I didn't need what I really didn't want. But I must admit I felt deprived not being able or willing or wanting to toss all caloric abandon to the cocoa-flavored winds and gobble down a disgustingly rich and sensuously gratifying serving of some sweet and heavy dessert. Some people can be so gluttonously reckless and I envy them. Most of them are younger than I, so I envy them even more. The younger they are, the more I envy them. Sometimes I envy them so much I hate them. I hate them so much I send the curse of fatness to their sweets-laden table. The curse flying to their face.

"Yes. Eat. Get fat. Die!"

In the big picture of life, it's disconcerting to think of the continuum of humankind from cute chubby infant to fat old codger. We are born fat, spend most of our adult life fighting the fat, and end up fatter than ever. The battle seems lost even before it is fought. With talk of the existence of fat genes, it probably is.

This situation in America has not only to do with our culture—the lure of ultra-sleek, anatomically incorrect bodies and the curse of idle minds—but also very much with the American diet, which, while improving, is undoubtedly one of the most bizarre and uninspired cuisines in the world. It is a most unhealthy cuisine with all of its animal meats and fatty ingredients. In fact, it is only the *reinvented* American cuisine which is considered healthy. One wonders if non-Americans find a fascination with hamburgers, pork chops, and apple pies as exotic, ethnic food. Undoubtedly so.

In our Chinese household, we assimilated American culture and traditions easily. We would eat Chinese food half the time and non-Chinese, that is, middle-American and Italian, the other half. One could count on the non-Chinese fare—tuna casserole or meatloaf with occasional spaghetti and pizza thrown in for ethnic flair. However, we could never count on the Chinese fare, except for the rice. Chinese cuisine has so many flavors, methods of preparation, spices, and ingredients. My mother used them all. And just look at all the provincial varieties. Variety is always the spice of rice. While rice never changed, every favorite Chinese dish of mine tasted a bit different each time. Meatloaf, on the other hand, always tasted like . . . well, meatloaf.

The Chinese cook with flavor built into the dishes while Americans cook something bland and tasteless to which one adds some equally bland brown gravy, creamy dressing, or bottled sauce to disguise the fact that the food has absolutely no taste. Not to insult the American houseperson, but a can of Alpo usually stimulates more taste buds than sliced white turkey with gravy—unless you throw in the canned cranberry sauce. It's no wonder if you see what goes into canned dog food versus turkey. Even dog food comes in more variety than sliced turkey. I couldn't stand American food day after day. I suppose tolerance has to do with what you are exposed to.

■   ■   ■

One thing about America: things are always changing. Somewhere between my infancy and childhood, they invented fast food. I was a little too young to catch the roller-skating drive-in craze, but I can distinctly remember walking into the first Burger King in our neighborhood—"Home of the Whopper." This Burger King seemed to be a comic book setting with its exaggerated primary colors and spick-and-span American atmosphere. To me, it wasn't even a real restaurant since it served only hamburgers—Whoppers and Junior Whoppers—the latter sounding like a contradiction in terms. Not even a hot dog. Everything came out with the efficiency of a returning bowling ball. Overnight, American cuisine was redefined and became synonymous with fast food, and never was middle age so easily threatened by the dreaded midriff bulge.

Once the McDonald's and White Castles proliferated, an even newer invention came to be: fast food drive-thrus! I was most aware of this phenomenon during my move to California while beginning my surgical residency in the late 1970s. It was natural that it should be in California, where grown adults will actually pay hard-earned money to walk up and down Stairmasters, those mechanized steps to nowhere, for hours on end but refuse to get out of the car to stuff their faces with burgers.

It seemed an insult to the human spirit and sense of self-worth not to at least get out of a car and exert some modicum of energy to waddle fifty feet to a counter and order a juicy Whopper. But to accommodate the slothfulness in all of us, under the guise of convenience and efficiency, fast-food drive-thrus became the beacon to all motorists. We'd drive five more miles not to have to climb out of our cars. Even the delivery side had become effortless. Forget the roller-skating waitress. Seated servers simply leaned out over the counter to hand us a bag of edible American history, expending only the tiniest of muscular activity.

Without a doubt this is the expected delivery system in America today. McDonald's used to proudly proclaim how many millions of burgers it had served. Now it is well into the billions. But the concept of fast food is as understandable as American cuisine in general. I'm sure I'm not alone when I wonder if I'm not the only idiot sitting in my car, engine running, radio playing, waiting impatiently for my fast food like a motorist caught in a traffic jam. Have I missed something or is fast food not supposed to take *all day* to serve?

Besides the fact that fast food often takes an extraordinarily long time to arrive, I am puzzled by the term itself. A linguist would have a field day. I suppose the "fast" refers to how it is prepared, that it should be ready before you even order. But then they should call it *precooked* food, which itself makes as much sense as preboarding an aircraft. Or, maybe it does refer to how quickly the food is delivered, from grill directly to mouth. Yet this is all so relative that as our lives and expectations pick up pace, fast is no longer fast enough. They should call it *sort-of-fast* food.

The "fast" could also refer to the food itself. But the only fast food I can think of are things like minnows and gazelles, or perhaps cod, before it becomes filet-o'-fish. *That's* fast food. Cows are not fast food. Idaho potatoes are dead slow.

Maybe those who call it "fast" food mean it to be like snack food or diet meals; that is, food you eat while fasting, which doesn't make any more sense than the term "noninvasive surgery." Anyway, a well-done, greasy, all-beef patty with cheese, lettuce, tomato, and mayo doesn't sound like food for a fast. If anything, only the tomato and, maybe, lettuce does. All in all, I think we're fooling ourselves. In reality, there is probably no such thing as fast food, just *relatively* fast food. And that is what life is all about. Relativity.

■   ■   ■

That said, much of this chapter has been written while I'm sitting in a convertible sports car, waiting for my fast food to be assembled, packaged, and delivered to my window. I realize that I'm now as lazy and slothful as any middle-aged professional. It's pitiful that inspiration and self-discovery must emanate from such a mundane setting. But then, I set out not so much to inspire, although that is a distant hope, as to tell the truth. And the truth is that even as life and your body change, so do perspectives. One day you are half dead. The next, you are half alive. Life is always trying to fool us into thinking or believing something that really isn't there. Like fast food. And I don't want to end up with a plate full of empty beliefs.

Think of Chef Boyardee. As kids, my sisters and I survived on food by Chef Boyardee. I don't know if there was ever such a person. I do know there is a picture of someone on the can of ravioli whom the owners would have us believe is him. I tend to doubt this because ever since I took my first mouthful of the canned red stuff, whether spaghetti and meatballs or cheese ravioli (they all tasted curiously the same), I've never *ever* met another Italian named Boyardee.

Back then, we all had the impression that spaghetti made you fat. All Italian women, except for Gina Lollabrigida and Sophia Loren, of course, were fat mamas. And nothing typified obesity as much as a lipid-bloated porker seated in front of a heaping plate of spaghetti with tomato sauce splattered all over his fat face and bulging shirt. So when we used to go to all-you-can-eat spaghetti night at Howard Johnson's, we always starved ourselves for days and left the restaurant feeling very guilty if not satiated—so guilty that we'd opt for all-you-can-eat fried chicken night the following week.

To show you what I mean about relativity, somewhere between my days at Howard Johnson's and now, somebody changed the name of spaghetti to pasta, christened it healthy, and made all athletes and half-starved models dependent on it. They took the guilt out of spaghetti and made it almost medicinal. Now it *is* what you eat when you're dieting. Marathoners with four percent body fat would feast on noodles for days prior to a race. Dainty ladies and worried middle-aged men like myself begin to order the stuff religiously as if the more you ate, the less you weighed—like cottage cheese—regardless of whatever else you shoved down your gullet. Somehow the only thing that happened to me is that I started to look more and more like a lipid-bloated porker. Only at this stage in life they call it "being successful." I can afford to lay down ten bucks for a plate of lo-fat carbs instead of twenty-nine cents for a can of Chef Boyardee. More for less. That'sa progress!

I must eat pasta or noodles in their various forms three or four times a week. I don't think I'm any less fat, but I must admit I do feel better, as if I'm doing my body a favor by eating pasta instead of a Whopper or Big Mac.

The struggle with food continues—what it means, what it is, what I want. Here I am, middle-aged, lipid-bloated porker, denying myself the things that came so reflexively as a child while giving in to the cultural trends and behavioral rationalizations of the times. Not getting any less bloated, certainly not any lighter in years. That's mid-life in a fat nutshell. The pulling back toward childhood and the pushing on of years—man-child in the promised waist land, beyond the reach of liposuction where a mere pound or two or three of fat is the difference between emotional discontent and contour bliss.

■   ■   ■

On most nights, feeling quite middle-aged, I reject the chocolate cake. However, on a particularly different night, I run, figuratively speaking, in my sports car to the nearest restaurant in my Beverly Hills neighborhood. Resisting the urge to drive an additional five miles to a local fast-food drive-thru on Sunset Boulevard, I park just outside the restaurant entrance. Before I go in, I do a quick, mostly symbolic, turn around the block on foot. Surely it was more than fifty feet this time—more like five hundred yards I tell myself. Well, that's good enough. Heart rate up a bit. One bead of well-deserved sweat. No guilt now. I take a table not more than ten feet from the dessert bin. I sit and watch the rack go round and round, carrying millions and millions of lipocyte-seeking calories. I scan the menu for the strawberry shortcake with the heavy strawberry syrup and heaping mound of whipped cream. Seeing none, I settle happily on a hearty slice of homemade apple pie. My favorite. A thick, sweet slice of Americana.

"Good choice," the waitress says. She would. She's thin.

"I'd like it warm."

"But, of course!"

No use denying myself now. Inhaling the aroma already.

"And make it big." Feeling the bolus slide seductively down my esophagus.

"À la mode?"

I plant both my hands firmly around my belly. I think of the billion prosperous people in China. "No," I say with regret, squeezing harder and harder, hoping the fat cells would die from the pressure. "No ice cream."

I sit, waiting patiently as my childhood goes round and round. I scan the room, hoping no one sees me. But everyone is eyeball-deep in food.

The slice arrives. It's big, spilling over the edges of the plate, daring me to indulge. I oblige, shoveling it into my mouth. It's warm. I taste its richness—all butter, all sugar, no skimping. Savoring its goodness, regretting nothing. Down to the last crumb.

I smile.

5

Fame

I was always a shy kid and thus never went fishing for fame. Fame scared me: the eyes of strangers peering at every pore of my face, dissecting each mannerisms. Never let them catch you with sweat on your brow or mucus in your nose. As it turned out, I was blessed with asthma, hay fever, *and* a very sensitive nose. Perfumes were as lethal as dust and a hearty laugh could produce paroxysms of life-threatening wheezing, so I was never a good candidate for fame. Yet like most mortals, I was fascinated by the concept—and, yes, the possibility—of it.

Life began as ordinary in Roslindale, there being nothing famous about the neighborhood except that it bordered Roxbury, the most notorious racial ghetto in Boston in the 1950s. Riots and Roxbury went together like rock-and-roll. For better or worse, my parents promptly moved from Roslindale to Quincy soon after my birth. Growing up in Quincy, named after the sixth president of the United States, was almost as good as growing up in Washington State as far as fame goes. Being a predominantly working-class suburb, we never knew celebrities except through radio, TV, newspapers, and magazines.

While my father was referred to as "a famous neurosurgeon" on many occasions—most notably when his name was printed in the city newspaper for getting slammed in a head-on collision, which landed him in the hospital and left most of his teeth scattered all over the South-east Expressway—I had always assumed, as little boys do, that he was truly famous. Little boys want their fathers to be famous. We expect it. Yet fame took on a different connotation back then. You see, Quincy and the city of Boston were my entire world; everybody I knew in this small world of mine knew my father. Likewise, I believed our whole family was famous, since we were the only Chinese—in fact, the only *Asian*—family in the whole neighborhood. People knew us. Everybody I knew seemed to know the Yuans!

Needless to say, this kind of fame didn't exactly spoil us in Quincy. It was a private kind of fame, an inward-facing fame. We felt famous even if we really weren't. We never had famous people for dinner. I didn't have famous friends to play with. No one in my elementary school sounded like they came from famous families. No Kennedys, Cabots or Lodges. For the most part, it was a life of ordinary fame: the kind that extended around the block, the kind that everyone has.

People, especially elders, treated me as special. Whether it was because I was smart, or fat, or Chinese, I never knew. I just felt special. I guess most kids at that age and time were treated—and wanted to feel—special. It gave us a perception and taste of fame, of being the center of attention. But part of my famously large ego thought I was *extra* special. Everyone else was just plain special.

I always got along with my elders, people of my parents' age or older, which at the time was really only the age I am right now. A sobering thought. I suppose my popularity with these elders had something to do with always being polite, never swearing, and never being wrong. Never. That seemed to set me apart.

I often became the teacher's pet, and being the only Chinese, the fat-test kid in the elementary school, and undoubtedly the brightest (or so the teachers always said), I became famous in my own right without really wanting to be or knowing what it was all about. It was a quiet fame, which sounds a bit oxymoronic but it isn't. Actually, it's the best kind of fame. I was treated as if I were famous and felt as if I were famous, without being or needing to act like I was famous. That's the kind of fame we need to instill in kids today. Private, quiet fame. Yet little did I realize the pre-carious position I was in: kids often hated the teacher's pet.

Of course, that wasn't real fame as we adults define it. But it did manage to give me a taste of how it felt to have someone other than my parents look at me with so much interest.

In school, it felt good to get so much attention for spelling large words, like "omniscient" and "onomatopoeia," and for multiplying ten pairs of four-digit numbers in less than a minute. For all my efforts, I don't think my neighbors knew I had such far-reaching talents. They would never have doubted it, but neither did they know for sure. Fame sometimes doesn't go beyond four walls.

As I think about it, there seem to be two distinct kinds of fame: one that is in your head and the other that is in the heads of others. We often consciously strive for the one, especially in the immature phase of life, but need the other, in the mature state of adulthood. Kids need to *feel* as if they're famous, but don't really need to be. Adults, for their own egos, *really* need to be, but often don't feel it. It's not uncommon that we get the two mixed up.

■   ■   ■

My fame was mostly in my head, in my dreams. My first encounter with real fame had to wait for the "Bozo the Clown" show. This was a decade before "Sesame Street" and a whole generation prior to "Teenage Mutant Ninja Turtles." But "Bozo the Clown," along with "Captain Kangaroo" and "Romper Room," was the big time for little tykes like me. My mother took my sisters and me to be on the "Bozo the Clown" show. Of course, I thought I was the only one who counted.

The studio was filled with cables running in every direction along the concrete floor. There were huge, movable cameras and a stage that looked like a circus ring surrounded by benches for the live audience to sit on and watch the show. The spotlights were unbelievably hot. The cameras were running. There was a surreal, larger-than-life feeling as I walked across the studio to shake Bozo's hand. The world quickly shrank to the size of a spotlight.

Right then, fame hit me in the head. It was a big deal to me. I couldn't believe that I was really on the "Bozo the Clown" show and thousands of households across Massachusetts were actually looking at me. The whole world gets compressed into a small space in front of a little kid's eyes. That is the nature of egocentrism.

Afterwards, I was more than a little perplexed and maybe a smidgen disappointed when no one but my neighbors commented on how wonderful I looked on TV. Surely someone else should recognize me—perhaps the school janitor or the mailman or even my barber. Well, at least my barber did. He was my father at the time.

But except for my barber, no one else said a word. Maybe I intimidated them. I learned that fame sometimes has that effect. Then again, it might have been that fame was still just in my head, still stuck within four walls. And that can satisfy for only so long. Oh, well—back to the sandbox.

Even if I wasn't famous after that show, Bozo the Clown was. He was the first celebrity I remember meeting. There was something to be said about that because, as everyone knows, fame has a tendency to rub off. People make such a big deal about Clinton and Kennedy. So fond memories and a smile cross my face whenever someone mentions Bozo the Clown, which people do every once in a while. Even though I'm not famous, Bozo the Clown still is. I can always brag that I was once on the "Bozo the Clown" show and hope that someone may remember. Unfortunately, the thing with Bozo is, he's just a clown. Since Bozo, I've had many brushes with fame.

The first famous politician I shook hands with was Governor Francis Sargent of Massachusetts, a kindly but distant Republican, which was probably some reasonable definition of a Republican back in the 1960s. I was chosen along with two other student musicians to pose with the governor for a Music Week promotional shoot. I was in junior high school back then and got all dressed up in my dark wool suit, the one I usually performed in because it looked so formal without being a real tuxedo. The wool tickled the hell out of my skin. Sometimes, I had to wear long pajama bottoms underneath so the wool trousers wouldn't cause my legs to itch. How I hated that.

Since I was a roly-poly kid, the suit fit tightly around my body. With some effort, I buttoned up all three front buttons and clipped on my matching tie. I must have looked pretty impressive, all dressed up for the governor. My elders and teachers would be proud. The walk through the state capitol with rows of marble busts and canvas portraits of all the important political figures I had read about in my American history books put the sobering thought in my mind, "I'm going to meet the Governor!" I felt big, self-important. To me, he was like the president of the whole world. He was important. Everyone knew his name—far more than even knew my father, that's for sure. He had aides all over. They greeted me and were nauseatingly wholesome and pleasant. They knew who I was and why I was there. All this made me feel pretty good, like a celebrity.

The governor came out and I was struck by how tall he was. That seems to be a common trait among famous people, being physically large. In reality, it is probably selective social discrimination against little people. It's easier for big people to step on little people in the climb to the top: easier to be noticed, easier to build self-confidence, easier to impress. I peered up at his face. I noticed he didn't sweat. And I wondered if he too was wearing pajamas under his wool suit.

Governor Sargent was well over six feet tall, certainly taller than most adults, who were, by definition, tall to any kid. His handshake was firm and professional, as if he did this all the time, which, of course, he did. He chatted with us a little, took a photo or two, and left. It was over in a flash.

That encounter did nothing to kindle any political ambition in me, but it did show me the lineage of power and fame, flowing down through years of heritage, one famous politician begetting another. From the founders of colonial New England, through American history, to the hands of Governor Sargent, into my palm. There is always a thread connecting obscurity with fame. It is rare for someone to be born into immediate fame and never be touched by commonality. Most famous people rise from common roots. More importantly, it showed me the humanness of fame that resides in real people—people you can actually shake hands with. Attaching fame to a person is only one discriminating way of looking at someone who may be quite common and ordinary.

By shaking the governor's hand, I had taken the first step toward demystifying fame. Seeing Senator Ted Kennedy in the late 1960s and 1970s did the same thing, especially after the assassination of his brothers. By then, he had risen to near-icon stature in Massachusetts and the nation. But he was still just as real and palpable as my father. At that time, I was not as aware as I am now of how a common man like myself relates to more powerful and famous people and what truths those relationships reveal about myself. The advantage of looking back is to pluck those pearls of truth and wisdom from each human embrace. More than fame itself, I'm always looking for those pearls.

Sometimes fame sneaks up on you and it is better to be oblivious to it. As a teenager, I happened to visit with cellist Yo-Yo Ma in his parents' New York apartment. His mother and my mother were schoolmates in Ginling College in China. It is not uncommon for Chinese parents to impress the importance of music upon their children. In fact, it is almost a truism to say that it is rare for Chinese *not* to play some musical instrument. I started violin lessons at age five because two other Chinese playmates of mine from nearby towns had started to take lessons. I didn't want to feel left out. Yo-Yo's sister is also an accomplished violist and pianist with whom I often played chamber music at Harvard Medical School. Both my sisters were budding pianists. That proves the truism.

During this brief visit, someone suggested that Yo-Yo and I play a duet. It was probably Yo-Yo's mother since she knew I played the violin and, like most Chinese mothers, assumed that I played better than I actually did. She probably expected me to be as good on the violin as Yo-Yo was on the cello.

For this occasion, his father lent me a petite Amati.* Had I known this violin was worth hundreds of thousands of dollars, I would have been more nervous. And had I known how famous Yo-Yo would become, I probably would have dropped the instrument. I would have been too intimidated to even tune it. Today, I would jump at the chance to play with him again, with or without the Amati. Not because it would give him much pleasure or that I wouldn't make a finger-tripping fool of myself. But just because I would hope that a little pearl would drop from his bow.

We did play a Beethoven duet: he, a true child prodigy; I, a spectator of fame, a pretender to greatness. While I can't say I remember any pearls from that experience—perhaps we did sound reasonably good— I can at least tell people that I once jammed with the world's greatest and most famous cellist, for that is what Yo-Yo is today. Everyone should be so lucky.

Years later, Yo-Yo would trail me at Harvard College. After medical school, I attended his concerts in Miami and Los Angeles, where I was taking my surgical residencies. A few words and handshakes were the extent of our friendship. We never had dinner together, never got beyond the

---

*Amati, along with Guarneri and Stradaveri, was acknowledged to be one of the three greatest Italian violin makers.

superficial cordialities that every common man exchanges each day, never again made music together. Despite similarities in our backgrounds, we belonged to different worlds. I continued to adore his musical sincerity. Like me, he played straight from the heart. Notes weren't just tones, pitches, rhythms and accents. They were nuances of emotion and soul. He reminded me of Ted Williams at the plate. Technically flawless, mentally engaged, emotionally unleashed. What I lacked most back then was technique. He is famous. I am not. Fame can also erect a barrier. That was a pearl.

Leonard Bernstein gave Yo-Yo his first big break at Carnegie Hall. I met Bernstein at Harvard when he was delivering a series of Norton lectures, masterfully entertaining and brilliantly scholastic expositions on the art of music. He vaguely remembered me at a Harvard benefit dinner in Beverly Hills many years later. It was one year before Bernstein's death, and all the high living and his advanced age had blurred his memory a bit. He seemed to love to reminisce, but the racking of his prodigious brain to match my obscure name with my equally obscure face was agonizing for him. Since I have this prejudice that people (usually non-Chinese people) are always mistaking me for some other Chinese, I suggested that before he split his brain thinking of who I was, perhaps he was thinking of Yo-Yo. Whereupon he immediately threw his head back, reaching his arms to heaven, and burst out for all to hear, "Who could mistake Yo-Yo?"

In my mind I completed the sentence ". . . and me?" Oh, just to be thought of by someone famous. . .

Actually, he swooned, "No one's like Yo-Yo! . . . OOHHHH!" hands flapping with enthusiasm and genuine adoration. Then, not having much to say about my name, Uncle Lenny proceeded to rave about my girlfriend and me being "such a gor-geous-looking couple. Just GORRR-GEOUS!"

I had to agree. Since I wasn't famous that evening, I might as well be good-looking. Gregory Peck said the same thing about the two of us later that year. O. J. Simpson and his then less famous wife, Nicole, volunteered a similar comment while licking ice cream cones at Baskin-Robbins. So Joanne and I ended up getting married. No use wasting a perfectly magnificent compliment from three of the world's most famous people.

If I could find a pearl in that evening of Bernstein prancing about, swooning, gesticulating, trying desperately to remember if he really knew who I was, it would be that being a little wild and flamboyant wasn't so bad if you wanted to be, or were already, famous. But being famous won't protect you from slowly losing your memory.

Leopold Stokowski, another wild and flamboyant celebrity conductor in his heyday, dropped me his own pearl when I was a member of an international youth orchestra playing in St. Moritz, Switzerland. He was the guest conductor and, when the orchestra messed up, he would chastise us, all the while wagging his baton.

"You can do better! You can do better!" he would scream at us, also with arms flapping.

Philosophically, I agreed with him. I always tried. But I didn't always succeed.

I found that if I pretended I was well-known to others, while not really being famous, I would put just enough pressure on myself to excel, to somehow justify my false fame. This was true in music, in studies, and in sports. Expectations can be wonderfully motivating to pretenders to fame. But it can also be devastating to those with real fame. I can't imagine Stokowski screaming at Yo-Yo in rehearsal.

■   ■   ■

At Harvard, you can easily believe that the universe revolves around this definitively famous institution. The sense of tradition is very strong. Great men and women have walked those hallowed halls. Some enter famous. Others leave famous. Listen to the parade of fame marching to the Crimson Tide: musicians like Piston, Ma, and Bernstein; writers like Emerson, Longfellow, Thoreau, James, and even Crichton; industrialists like Rockefeller and Hearst; politicians like Adams, Roosevelt, and Kennedy (*all* the Kennedys).

There was George Wald, Nobel Laureate for medicine, big-time scientist, and my advisor while an undergraduate biology major at Harvard College. Professor Wald reinforced my initial intimidation by fame. His world-wide renown as a scientist-turned-peacenik preceded my matriculation at Harvard. Visiting his office was like visiting a spiritual guru. The overcluttered room, filled in every corner and on every surface with stacks and stacks of books, articles, letters, notes, journals, and molecular models, conjured up images of how Albert Einstein's office might have looked. His long, flowing gray hair made his legendary image instantly recognizable. He looked the part of fame. He thrived on fame and its controversy. His science was revolutionary, his politics were radical, his philosophy eclectic, his social etiquette entirely individualistic. He was different. The only thing ordinary about Professor Wald was his wardrobe.

At Harvard Medical School there was Dr. Joseph Murray, general surgeon-turned transplantation surgeon-turned plastic surgeon, who first opened my mind and heart to plastic surgery. He demonstrated that plastic surgery was not merely a technical dexterity, but problem-solving with applied anatomy. He, too, would be awarded a Nobel Prize in medicine for his pioneering work in transplantation. A hard-working, thoughtful, but soft-spoken man, he showed me that fame and brilliance didn't preclude niceness; also, that otherwise seemingly ordinary guys needn't toil in oblivion. Fame can come even to those who don't seek it.

I finished my plastic surgery training with one of the world's most respected and famous plastic surgeons, Dr. D. Ralph Millard, Jr., also a Harvard Medical School graduate, from whom pearls fell like raindrops from heaven. His insights about life and living were just as valuable to me as his tips on plastic surgery. For the first time, I began to see how most things in life, especially in plastic surgery, combined to form a paradigm of life itself. The struggle between beauty and blood supply was symbolic of the struggle between success and failure. Boldness in surgery was not unlike boldness in war. Aesthetic concepts were as diverse as political beliefs. And fame, in as competitive a field as plastic surgery in its early days, was as ready to knock one off the pedestal as much as it was poised to place one on it.

Armed with a head full of pearls, I moved to California where encounters with fame are commonplace, reaffirming the humanness of fame. There is no telling when fame will walk through the doors of my office and lay his or her body on my operating room table. Many have and, for all their outward fame, people still bleed and heal the same.

Yet there is a difference between the famous environs of East Coast intellectualism and the equally famous milieu of West Coast celebrity. The superficial issue of fame in Hollywood becomes associated with the poignant concern of self-worth. If you are famous, other famous people notice you, and ordinary people stare and ask for autographs. If you aren't, you can't get a good table at Morton's (the ultimate in power restaurants, where the Hollywood high and mighty go to be seen, schmooze, and maybe even to eat). Actually that's not entirely true. I once did eat at Morton's a decade and a half ago when I first moved to Los Angeles and sat at a great table right around the corner from the entrance. I could see everyone and everyone could see me and wonder who this Chinese guy was, chomping on his nine-dollar cheeseburger right out there in the open. Little did I know that anyone who was anyone didn't sit at this table right around the corner from the entrance.

Since I was so ignorant, it is more than my self-consciousness about fame that prevents me from returning to Morton's. In fact, it's the embarrassment of actually being able to get a decent seat and to afford the steep prices but still having people wonder who is that graying Chinese guy with the double chin and early midriff bulge munching on his Caesar salad. I suppose that all these encounters with famous people instilled an expectation of fame at some point in life and, along with it, a sense of failure for not having achieved it myself.

Granted, any good parents would rather bask in the glory of their own sons and daughters, no matter how illusory, than to be adored by a sea of faceless, nameless people. But at some point, even that won't be enough. It's just human nature. The humanness and commonness of fame experienced over four decades of life makes it all attainable. Being attainable makes it worse.

When something is attainable and desirable, we have to ask ourselves why we don't have it. I ask that of myself every day I look in the mirror only to find more and more space between my graying hairs and, perhaps, even between my ears. The answer may be that it's less attainable than we think. This tears at the root of my abilities. It is akin to admitting failure. And *that* I couldn't do, even if I had no hair at all. The other answer is more palatable; that is, we don't desire it enough. And that is because there lies the dilemma of fame. Contrary to Andy Warhol's well-known adage, fifteen minutes of fame is not always fame. It may be infamy.

I often walk alone in the hills above Beverly Hills, lost in my private thoughts. Sometimes I'm inspired. Sometimes I'm brooding. But I'm always honest. Along may come a wave of that illusory fame, a second of self-indulgent pretending. I remember Bozo the Clown. I wish I were Yo-Yo. Does fame beget importance and meaning, or is it the other way around?

Here comes a tour bus, Movieland or Star Tours, looking at the homes of the rich and famous. They drive by my house overlooking the canyon below. The passengers gaze longingly out the tinted windows, mesmerized by their imaginations, thrilled by the expectation of fame so close at hand. They are hoping to see someone. Anyone . . . even me. I indulge them with my private joke by pulling down my sunglasses and looking away. If I am in my car, I tuck my head low, pull down the visor and race away, as if annoyed by their intrusion into my neighborhood. I become inaccessible. They can always debate who it was they saw and go home murmuring among themselves how neat it was to catch a glimpse of that famous actor from that great film about something or other. Or maybe it was that up-and-coming comedian What's-His-Name. I know that if I had been sitting in that tour bus twenty years ago—which I did—I would have done that and felt it was exciting. And I did. And it was.

But I am not that famous actor. Nor am I that new comedian. I am not even that most well-known, prominent Beverly Hills plastic surgeon to the stars or a father whom people all around the neighborhood know. Only one person has ever asked for my autograph and he is now dead. The last time my picture was in the newspaper was when I got married and my brand-new, good-intentioned, obviously proud mother-in-law probably would have had to pay the publisher to print it had it not been a community service and tradition to do so. The next time my picture gets published will probably be when I die, if I'm lucky.

The bus is gone. I am alone again. In the quiet, I realize that the only person, outside of my family, who really knows me—whom I *really* care to know me—is me. It was fun to have had that little joke, but they'll never know what happens on the other side of their tour bus window.

■ ■ ■

I do not regret that I am not famous, truly famous. It's enough to have tasted it. Fame is like fish. It is only when it is caught that it becomes a trophy. You can spend a lifetime pursuing it only to find that often the most unsuspecting and least experienced person catches it. And if that is all that you ever want out of life; if it's your *only* pursuit and trophy worthy of living, once you have caught it, in time it will begin to putrefy—just enough perhaps to make you want to throw it back, occasionally enough to overwhelm your good senses. Even if you haven't caught it, stay near enough, often enough, long enough and the smell will soon permeate indelibly. It might even be enough to kill some.

When I fish, I like to throw in the bait or jiggle the lure, sit back, and enjoy the water's bejeweled surface. If I come up empty-handed as on most of my excursions, I will have enjoyed the breeze on my face and the water on my flesh, and perhaps have caught something more of life, even if it is only in my head. If a fish is lucky enough to be hooked by me, it will struggle bravely, as I will too. I'll reel it in, all by myself, admire its shiny scales and well-designed shape. If it is worthy, I'll take a photograph and then let it go at that. That's all. It will live to become someone else's trophy. You won't ever catch me strutting a string of fish around my neck because no one wants to see the same dead fish every single day.

6

Soft Balls

As you know by now, baseball was a big part of my boyhood. I learned how to slide in Little League. It looked so easy the way the pros did it. It actually looked like fun. But once I had to try it in person, I was sure I was going to break a leg or skin the hide off my butt.

At first, I didn't know the physics of a slide and it took me a while to learn why and when one should slide. I felt as if I were falling, not sliding. I soon found out that it was important to get up a head of steam, to get enough momentum, so that when you lay out your leading leg and slide on your hip, you skim the dirt instead of plopping into it. I always dreaded the slide because I thought I was too fat—sort of like trying to skip a boulder across a lake.

The secret to gaining enough momentum as a Little Leaguer is to abandon all fear. Being game enough to try to slide at all is the first significant step. You've got to be confident and self-assured, and act like it even if you're not. Getting to the base is all that matters. You can't be timid when trying to score on a slide. That's a sure way to get hurt, or to get thrown out.

In junior high, we were taught to be even more aggressive in our offensive base-running. We learned how to "take out" an infielder by running dead at him with the hope of blocking his vision or causing him to flinch just enough to prevent a play. We'd aim our slide toward his feet, not to intentionally spike or hurt him, but to get him to lose concentration, to make him react with a false step which might interrupt his throwing rhythm. You couldn't worry about getting your front teeth knocked out by the attempted throw to first. I did my share of sliding then. I practiced and played hard, but fair.

Even as a pitcher I tried to think aggressively. The hard, tightly woven leather baseball was just as much of a weapon to me as it was a target for the batter. As a batter, and a good one at that, I knew that once you feared the pitcher, became intimidated by his stare or stance on the mound, or thought about getting hit by a seventy mile-an-hour fastball aimed at your head, you were as good as out. You can't bail out just because you might get beaned by a wild pitch. You've got to learn how to dig in. As a batter, I countered my pitcher's knowledge with a thirty-six-inch bat—a hell of a big sucker for a twelve-year-old. Most pitchers were only four feet tall themselves and I knew that bat looked like a tree trunk from forty-five feet away.

As a pitcher, as much as I tried to throw strikes, I didn't mind throwing a little hard and inside just to keep the batter honest. It wasn't uncommon that this tactic would lead to a few extra bases on balls. But I wasn't shaken by that. As a lefty, I had a great move to first base and, more often than not, was able to pick the runner off, so I'd let my pitches fly.

Being aggressive didn't come naturally. I had to learn its advantages. In fact, I was, and still am, a pacifist at heart. I want everyone to get along, to be happy, and to have a good time. Most kids are decent and instinctively feel the same way. Sports allowed us—even demanded—aggressive behavior because that's often what it took to win. We all liked to win.

My aggressiveness in sports did not extend to the social arena. In my whole life, I remember only one legitimate fight I was in where punches were thrown. It happened in junior high school.

Junior high is always a tough time. It's when boys begin developing their masculine characteristics: dating pretty girls, pestering the teacher, and beating the shit out of fellow classmates. We had fights all the time. It was always fairly predictable who was going to fight whom after school. It fact, it was expected. Some students probably looked at it as extracurricular activity. Kids easily lost standing with their fellow classmates if they didn't show up for the fisticuffs.

Every junior high has its self-designated aggressive males whose only homework seems to be beating up on someone after classes in the bushes at the edge of the ball field. Some of them might have graduated from hand-to-hand combat to Uzis or other semi-automatic weapons by now. Worse still, maybe they're IRS agents.

I was never involved in any of these slug fests and really couldn't understand the point or value in it. I'd much rather show up a guy by beating him two out of three in a game of chess or stealing a girl away by befriending her with chewing gum. I always carried a pack of chewing gum in my shirt pocket.

But boys do need to establish their manliness early in life, not so much because it is all that important to be able to break someone's jaw or even necessary to stand up to someone physically rather than intellectually, but because it is just that much more difficult later on in life to gain that experience. It is the symbolism of the gesture which is important and not so much the ability to form a fist. Somehow I can't imagine a grandfather getting into his first altercation at age seventy.

I used to walk to school or ride the bus carrying a violin case during the days we had orchestra practice. I dreaded those days since I knew I looked like a geek. During those painful days, I conjured up images of gangsters with their violin cases, pretending I, too, had a Tommy gun with which I'd do away with anyone who dared tease me. When I didn't feel *that* aggressive, I pretended I was a virtuoso, a man of importance, someone who couldn't care less about what people—especially dumb, talentless, bull-headed people—thought. I didn't get teased much despite my fear. Maybe that proved the effectiveness of these mind games. The ability to cope, in the face of imagined adversity, toughened me more than any real rumble in the park.

However, that one time in every boy's life finally came. It wasn't at all without meaning like most of the stupid, senseless fights. It might have even changed my whole life. As you've probably gathered by now, I was rather meek and mild as a child, more apt to fits of cerebral fantasy than fits of physical rage. Through most of my early years in junior high school, I was aware of a particularly pig-headed student (and I use the term "student" loosely since I don't imagine he ever truly studied, although to give him credit, he didn't drop out or kill anyone either). He used to call me "chink" which I took as an insulting term for what I was—a Chinese. At that time in my life, the novelty had worn out a bit. I can't say I was either ashamed or especially proud of being Chinese. It was just what I was, like being a boy. I didn't feel that much different from many of the other students, so it was quite a jolt to me when he called me "chink." I wasn't insulted initially, just sort of surprised he would even bother to identify me as something other than just another junior high kid who happened to be a geek. I would have been less puzzled if he had called me "brain" or "fatso."

At any rate, it dawned on me that it was rather annoying to be called "chink," not because the word conjured up any demeaning images (I was too naive and couldn't understand what "chink" had in common with being Chinese), but because it was obvious that he meant it in some disrespectful way, designed to put me down or provoke me. It's not so much what one is called, but how it's intended.

By this time, I had graduated from geek to well-rounded geek. I had gone from a rather rotund and flabby 180 pounds to an athletic 165 pounds by dieting and playing three sports in school: baseball, football, and basketball. This student-goon happened to be on the same varsity football team. While I was a respectably robust right guard, he was the largest offensive tackle the school had. In fact, he was the biggest kid in the whole damn school at six feet and nearly two hundred pounds. Most of all, he was a tough prick.

We were in the boy's locker room where a good 50 percent of the challenges take place. We were getting dressed for a wrestling class. Being two or three years younger than other classmates, I was not as physically endowed as I suspected many of the other boys were at this early stage of life and always felt a bit self-conscious and intimidated in the locker room. I was pretty fed up by now with this guy's attitude and constant taunting. When he called me "chink" this time, I couldn't ignore him. So I asked him, probably very politely, to take it back. Now, that, of course, is the stupidest thing to ask a prolific teenage goon to do. I mean, how many bullies do you know take back an insult in front of three dozen of his peers in the boy's locker room? Perhaps if I had asked him more academically what exactly he meant by the word "chink" things might have turned out differently. But I didn't and so they didn't.

He said no. Of course.

I said, "Take it back." This time more emphatically.

He said, "No, *make* me."

Not being too creative under pressure, I reiterated in my most emphatic voice. "Take it back, I said." Apparently I wasn't convincing enough.

Undaunted, he said, "Go ahead. Take the first swing." He even stuck out his chin.

I thought this rather unfair, so I said no. Then I said the second stupidest thing. "*You* take the first sw . . ."

Of course I ended up on the floor before I could close the quote. I remember being brought into the coach's office, nose bloodied, head floating somewhere up in the gym rafters. I was too stunned to cry.

After close consultation with his assistant, the coach felt it would be interesting to have me wrestle the bully in class. Today, a suggestion like that would be grounds for calling a civil rights attorney. But I'm sure my brain was more than a bit rattled. All the other kids were surprised I had stood up to the guy so I couldn't let them down. I said the third stupid thing in less than ten minutes.

"Okay. I'll wrestle."

The coach thought my speed might be a match for the bully's strength. Wrong.

I got pinned in under a minute with thirty of my classmates looking on. But two things happened that day. One, I learned to respect myself and to be proud of being Chinese, of being who I was and what I thought and what I felt. And two, I never got called "chink" again. *Ever.*

Life would be great if the story ended in junior high school. But something happened in the meantime. Twenty-five years have passed and I've not had a single other opportunity to fight again. Having lived all those intervening years in urban areas such as Boston, Miami, and Los Angeles, some might call me lucky. I've never fired a gun and hope I never will. As for domestic battles, I'd just as soon walk away from an altercation with a woman as argue with her. I know that I've become a little more fearful of heights. I hate roller coasters and, despite the comfort of having my well-trained hands in someone else's anesthetized flesh during surgery, I can't bear the thought of baiting my own hook.

I do play ball on Wednesday nights—not baseball, just softball. I'm on a team in a city league with other middle-aged men who probably have punched out a few people and have fired a pistol. I agreed to play because half of the team was composed of other doctors I knew, and I thought it would be a relaxing experience. Besides, I loved playing baseball in my youth.

But these guys are the serious types. They yell obscenities at each other, throw hard, take losing seriously, and wear spikes. The most telling sign of all is that they slide.

I haven't slid into a base for decades. I mean, I still know how to slide. It's like batting or throwing. You still know the mechanics, the theory, the nuances. It doesn't leave you after all those formative years. But I don't relish the thought of having to slide. I definitely don't want to slide. My fingers are too valuable and my skin too thin. I have two bulging discs and my sphincter muscles aren't as strong as they used to be. I'm thirty pounds heavier and twenty-five years wiser. While I want to win as much as the next guy, I won't slide.

Don't ask me how I arrived at that decision. We all start to give up certain pleasures of our youth. Some are not physically possible. Some are no longer enjoyable. Some were just plain stupid in the first place, like Chinese fire drills in the middle of a busy boulevard. Most, one way or another, strike at the very core of our individual souls, manifesting the development of a unique person. Each of us shapes himself or herself as a human being as if we were Christmas trees, selectively hanging and removing ornaments to give each tree a different character and a different appeal.

There have been times when I stood on first base, staring intently at second, thinking what I would do if the play at second was close. I mentally go through the lessons I had learned as a kid, picturing my leading leg hitting the bag and breaking up a double play with a spray of dirt. I debate the merits of a hook slide or hand tag. I think about how important it is to play at the same level as my peers, not to embarrass myself or act unmanly by not sliding. Just being out on the baseball diamond—even if the pitcher's mound is fifteen feet closer to home and the bases are thirty feet closer together, even if the pitches are slow and arching, not high and tight—and having a leather glove on and a bat in hand brings back the glory days of youth and the time I stood up to the school bully.

I've always prided myself on having the desire to win, to give it my all. There is so much to gain if only you're not afraid. Coming into the mid-portion of a life, I think it important to recharge all the positive forces and components of life and not slip into mediocrity and complacency. I try to keep my body in shape, but I do realize my genetic and physical limitations. I accept the fact that the body shape is constantly changing. I want to keep my mind open and absorbent, always on edge, always a bit skeptical. Young.

Unfortunately, one thing I cannot get myself to do is slide.

I get down on myself because I *do* feel scared. I don't want to skin my thigh or bruise my butt. I know what that is like and it isn't fun. I don't want to risk tearing my sweatpants like I once did in Little League, exposing my delicate flesh and soiled underwear to the whole world. I think this is all so stupid because it isn't such a big deal and because everyone else slides. I feel myself go soft.

I have been defeated by age. I have been humbled by fear. I spit into the ground and sense my manhood leak out of my body. If only we were playing fast pitch hardball. I wish I had it in me to beat the shit out of the second baseman. Of course, I never would.

I dig into the meaning of this as I do with most things which appear to be most trivial. I juggle my masculinity in my mind. Out of the self-critical deflation comes a face-saving thought. Better soft balls than a soft mind. Better soft balls than a tough prick. Better soft balls than no balls at all.

This week a fellow middle-aged softballer, one who *would* slide in a game and who yells in disgust when we are losing (which is often), but who is the nicest, most congenial person off the field, made near-contact with a base-runner while he was playing catcher. It wasn't his normal position (second base or shortstop was). The score wasn't close, and the runner didn't even slide.

For that split second of fate when multiple forces come together, like getting called "chink" by the school bully in the boy's locker room for the last time in one's life, or swinging the bat at blinding speed to meet with precise exactness the seventy-mile-an-hour white, leather ball spinning faster than you can count—in that split second your life can change and you can't explain how things happen. They just do. In that split second when competitiveness and chance meet, my friend, bracing for the impact that never came, fell to the ground and, with a sudden jerk of his neck that caused the spinal cord to mash itself against an all-too-tight bony canal, became a quadriplegic. Life had become a disaster.

I go back to the one fight of my life. There must have been a reason for that one and only encounter with a fist. Whether it be rationalization, reality, or defense mechanism, I understand why I don't slide. It is because I choose not to slide. I don't need to prove anything to anyone, including myself. I did that when I was twelve.

■   ■   ■

It was the bottom of the last inning. We had been losing the game since the first inning. Our determination and a lucky bounce brought us back to a tied game. There were two outs already and we were riding high on a stunning comeback. There were no spectators in the stands. It was just their team and ours. I singled convincingly into center, and as I stood on the first base bag looking toward second, the next batter stepped up to the plate. I leaned toward second and spit into the dirt. I dug my foot into the base to get a good pushoff. I didn't want to be the last out.

The batter smashed the softball past the shortstop and I took off for second. As I rounded second, I saw the ball roll past the left-fielder on a bad hop. This was my opportunity, everything was on the line. Hope and dread rushed through my aging body. I sprinted toward third and was waved home by the third-base coach.

"He's crazy!" I thought as I turned the corner. I knew from the speed of the ball and the speed of my feet that a play at the plate was a distinct possibility.

I headed for home, the fate of the game resting heavily on my middle-aged head. I felt my hamstrings burn. I could see the catcher set up to receive the throw. The debate of slide or no slide poured through my mind. The desire to win and be manly clashed loudly with the common sense of self-preservation.

"You're the hero. Slide, man, slide!"

"You're smarter than all these guys. Save your precious skin!"

Hard ball at twelve was different than softball at thirty-eight. I felt my fingers form a fist. The catcher was crouched dead ahead, mitt wide open, feet firmly planted. I heard the ball behind me. I churned my legs faster, my eyes locked onto home plate. Time to be the hero.

The ball whizzed discernibly past my left ear. The catcher moved quickly to his right for the ball. In a split second, I chose "no slide." At the moment the ball smacked into the catcher's mitt, I twisted my body and neatly avoided the tag. I stepped on home. We won the game. Both my pride and my pants were intact.

I love softball.

7

Burning Leaves

Whenever traveling in China, I am struck by the multitude of odors: the sting of acrid smoke generated by the use of coal, the garlicky richness of Chinese food in each three-ring alley of every circus city street, the fetid stench of too many human beings in one place at one time. It all makes for a sense of "strangeness." A foreign world.

As I inhale my surroundings, I become awed by the perspective that I am walking "upside-down" on the "other side" of the world so very far from "home."

It is 1992, and I am at a worn and dingy hotel (incredibly, but reliably, touted to be the city's best). It is located by the concrete shores of man-made Lake De-Chou in Shantung province. I am in this city operating on Chinese patients as part of a life-long program between me and all the world. Mine, like many, is a life of delicate balance between stability and restlessness, surgical triumph and medical disaster, blessings and guilt, foreignness and familiarity, future dreams and past experiences.

I have spent a few weeks each of the last seven years crusading in four underdeveloped countries on a dozen different occasions, donating my American-educated skills as a plastic surgeon to underserved areas, searching, perhaps, for a little redemption for the inordinate blessings bestowed upon me throughout life. To sacrifice and to suffer, to paraphrase

70

my father, makes one feel a little more worthy and appreciative of life. It is the yin-yang of life.* Without the yin, you can hardly expect to appreciate the yang, or vice versa. Without the versa, you can't appreciate the vice.

It is always more rewarding when these various trips involve more danger, harsher conditions, more difficult cases, and, more importantly, greater personal sacrifice. The farther I get from home in the United States the better. I've worked in Honduras in Central America during the surreptitious Contra-gate years and in the Philippines during the massacre at Malacanang Palace in the tumultuous year immediately following the dramatic fall of the Marcos regime. I have been to China, land of the inscrutables, on four previous excursions, forever intrigued by the immense changes each time.

My first visit was in 1975. The country and its people, including all my relatives there, were caught in a time warp. China was truly isolated from Western civilization. The rest of the world was marching forward but China had dived back into its paranoiac shell, which was just beginning to crack. I was too young at the time to understand the true significance of the movement called the Cultural Revolution. Apparently, neither did many others until years later. Suffering was the norm then, especially for the educated class. One of my father's sisters, a music teacher, was sent into the countryside to work the rice fields. She spent all of her waking hours hunched over the fertile soil, planting the life-giving stalks, such that years later, when all was done, she was unable to stand erect, her back so curved she couldn't look at the sky. The revolution had killed my maternal grandfather, my namesake, the former Presiding Bishop of the Anglican Church. He, like many members of the five reactionary classes of people, was refused medical treatment for his bleeding ulcer after having been placed under house arrest by the Red Guards. One of his family's closest friends, a medical doctor, looked on helplessly, the threat of political and physical retribution too great to overcome, refusing to come to his aid or ease his pain.

In 1983, traveling alone, I met scores of the intelligentsia: writers,

*According to Confucian philosophy, the universe is in cosmological harmony with various elements and forces balancing each other in all spheres of a symmetric life. Like two sides of a coin, one cannot exist without the other. The yang is masculine, active, hot, hard, and light, while the yin is feminine, passive, cold, soft, and dark.

conductors, religious leaders, actors—all caught in a time warp within a time warp, battling a government-designated disease called "spiritual pollution." The opening of China to Western influences after the downfall of the Gang of Four threatened the uniformity which kept the people under control. It was hard to think that someone like me could really be a threat to China. Individually, it was absurd. As an influx, China's gates now flung irreversibly open by détente, it was almost certain. People can be suppressed, but ideas cannot. Paranoia had paralyzed the body but primed the mind for the coming revolution. My relatives, imbued with the same strange sense of fear and paranoia resulting from having lived through those difficult years, marveled at the access I had to these potentially "dangerous" elements, whom I met in crowded parks, private cafes, and dark hotel rooms. I definitely felt out of my element.

That inevitable revolution came swiftly in 1989. I was transfixed by the events in Beijing: the tanks; the masses who could have been my friends and relatives; the intelligentsia calling out for democratic change; the invisible, yet all-controlling, government which hovered like a thick shroud, waiting to snuff out the sparks of that change.

Now, three years after the infamous and bloody Tiananmen incident, the government leadership itself seemed once again to be entrapped in its own time warp as most of the country embraced previously condemned Western ideas such as capitalism, free-market enterprise, rock-and-roll, and cosmetic surgery, leaving Communist ideals by the wayside. China appeared hellbent on the future. If ever there was a place where the future collides with the past, it is in China. That was the lesson this time around.

■   ■   ■

This particular trip stirred a host of emotions in me. I was conscious of standing at my own life's crossroads, having passed what was probably the mid-point of my life. My father and his brother (along with a half dozen of his close childhood classmates and cousins) were traveling together to their hometown in Ningpo along the coast of the South China Sea. They were in search of my father's dilapidated home buried deep within the bustling bowels of this busy seaport city.

We gathered together in old Shanghai and took a rusting steamliner along the coast, sleeping twelve to a room in smoke-filled berths. The berths reminded me of foreign prison blocks seen in countless movies where masses of strangers coughed, sneezed, and breathed on each other, waiting unknowingly for death or freedom to knock on their door. Those who couldn't afford the bunk-beds slept on the cold, hard floor in the exposed hallway. My father's group spent most of the time huddled by the railing, reminiscing about China and their past, when being poor and unworldly only meant that their friendship and family life were all the more rich and necessarily self-sufficient. They looked out into the blackness of the sea and saw the stars dancing off the waves, eagerly waiting for the familiar lights of the city in the distance. It was their laughter that broke the darkness of the past.

I was in the enviable position of chronicling this remarkable reunion. An outsider of sorts, I looked for significance—a truth—in every twitch of their consciousness, every encounter with their past. They had come back to this city a few years before, but could not find the house. Whole neighborhoods had been rearranged and entire streets were lost. This time, with the help of a local classmate, a chain-smoking professor of Chinese history who himself spent thirteen years in a prison during the Cultural Revolution, they finally came face to face with the old compound.

My father gave a small yell of recognition when he saw the brick wall. The familiar gateway to their home had been sealed over, but we could clearly see the outline of the original doorway in the skewed orientation of the individual bricks. Thick coats of white paint couldn't hide the telltale pattern. Unable to pass through, unlike the thousands of times long ago, they were forced to enter through a side walkway.

I could see the joy in all their eyes as they crossed the threshold and strolled into the crowded compound where buildings had hardly changed but memories and occupants had. The orchard, once beautiful and filled with fruit trees, seeming larger to them then when they were little children, had seen the ravages and inhumanity of war, the memories of playful frolicking giving way to visions of horrible executions carried out in the heat of civil war. As children, they hadn't understood why their world was changing. As adults, they still couldn't believe it had. No wonder this land, so stained with the blood of fellow countrymen, grew no trees or grass, but was left barren with the dust of the inner city, fertilized only with the transparent hope of a captive people. The small room on the first floor of the house appeared half as large as they had imagined and both my father and uncle marveled at their modest beginnings. I reflected: this was where half the seeds of our life in America were planted.

The face of the past stared unrelentingly at my father and uncle. They scampered playfully around the compound walls and joked, like the little children they once were, about memories of this place and of times together, gathering at their grandfather the bishop's house nearby. They talked of Sunday lunches with all their relatives and running to school hand in hand. They chuckled about picking watermelon seeds to sell as dried delicacies and catching lucky grasshoppers to keep as pets. They tried to remember each doorway, each beam, each step. But tears of sadness and longing lurked ever solemnly just beneath their thinly veiled laughter.

They felt the strangers in their home. The current occupants of the house, though cheerful and friendly, were not of their blood. The oversized clay urns, once proudly guarding the entrance to the bishop's house, lay broken and half-filled with lifeless grains of sand. The river which used to flow so freely just outside their schoolyard was now a frozen stream of concrete. The nave of the church where they worshiped each Sunday, where their grandfather taught the words of God, was now a neglected warehouse of outdated, rusted machinery, itself once productive of mostly utilitarian items like tools and furniture rather than of spiritual healing. Though they talked of ways to restore the buildings and grounds to their past glories, all knew they spoke only empty words. Who says you can't go home? It just may be too painful; the past had devoured their home.

Amid the nostalgia that pervaded this tightly knit group of relatives, I saw in my father a sense of searching for the future. He had traveled to Ningpo not only to seek out his roots, but, like me, to offer his assistance to his hometown as a neurosurgeon. He had retired from a very successful practice a year ago, but found that he could not completely leave something which had consumed forty years of his life. He was working part time as chief of neurosurgery for a Veteran's Administration hospital in Boston as well as a consultant for the Massachusetts General Hospital. But his dream was always to return to China, to give something back to the country he had left behind over forty years ago and which had inspired him, not because of what it had, but because of what it lacked at the time—well-trained neurosurgeons. I sensed not only a satisfaction and self-compelling need in his return, but also a guilt, of being blessed beyond all those left behind.

It is difficult to put myself exactly in his place, to feel what it's like to return home, welcomed and respected, yet not fully connected to that vestigial homeland. There were still-recognizable classmates and some familiar city sites. The medical community embraced him, enticing him to return to work in their newly built hospital. But this homecoming was different; it was not the jubilant triumph of World War II soldiers, or the hostile indifference of returning Vietnam vets. There was something much more profound and ambiguous, like a smell one cannot put one's finger on. He thought he could join with them, to educate, to serve. He was wrong.

With the embrace, there was a sense of subdued resentment. With the acknowledgment of humility came a defensive aloofness. With the desire to give and receive, there was a hesitant opportunism to possess and exploit what was being given. The pride of having an American-trained doctor visit the new hospital brought prestige and advantage to local doctors who hosted this visit. Yet we seemed to be more of a trophy, brought home to shine light upon these doctors in the eyes of more powerful local officials.

As my father spoke to the hospital officials and chiefs of services about how he could be of service, there was an unspoken uneasiness. Two lovers in an illicit, guarded embrace. Neither too vulnerable nor too aggressive. Both cautious with a fear of being hurt, a fear of hurting. They might have started out life together in this city, but now they were truly from opposite ends of the earth. In the end, the passion was left unconsummated to await a future détente. I could see the unrequited longing in my father's eyes. Seventy years of living and he couldn't even go home.

■   ■   ■

I left my father and his group in Shanghai, allowing them to digest their experience, and headed north to do my own work. Lectures on reconstructing misshapened heads and full days of operating on patients with congenital deformities of the lips and palates made for a productive week. I've learned in my international travels that, no matter where you are, everyone appreciates the value and beauty of restoring a human being to normal form and function. In countries where people have less, they appreciate you even more. But the satisfaction of education and surgical accomplishment on this particular trip mixed with the uncomfortably incomplete events of the Ningpo homecoming.

Throughout this week, I was guest of honor at nightly banquets, not the usual ten or twelve courses we are accustomed to in America, but at least twenty or even twenty-four dishes of various delicacies: fried scorpions hunted from beneath the rocks on nearby Tai Shan mountain, cold shredded jellyfish, dried donkey dick, and sauteed cattle's cock from animals seen grazing along the countryside. Tradition had anointed all of these with the essence of virility and strength. Needing to be empowered as such and not willing to offend my hosts, I enthusiastically devoured my share of every dish presented.

Each delicacy was an experience. The scorpions were crunchy on the outside, while moist, salty, and not all that unpleasant on the inside. The donkey's dick and cattle's cock were . . . well . . . what you might expect, I suppose.

As I feasted on the never-ending parade of adventurous, if not delicious, cuisine, I couldn't help wondering what happened to all those starving Chinese for whom I cleaned off my plate as a chubby child. Every guest sitting around the crowded table certainly appeared well fed. And each new aromatic surprise brought flashes of this little Chinese kid stuffing himself with life.

The nightly gorging rituals would have been enough except that the Shantung native's favorite and most formidable sport was not eating, but drinking. One hundred seventy-proof rice wine mixed with red wine and local beer soon had me gasping for air and unbuckling my belt. I was never a big drinker, even though I had my first taste of beer at two.

As a teenager, I always walked the straight and narrow. I'd never developed a taste for alcohol, never got drunk, never felt a "macho" or peer pressure "thing." Basically lived a pretty boring life as far as partying went. So the nightly gorge-fests and drinking parties, which were a necessary part of my welcoming reception, left me feeling physically unhealthy, although, in a sense, spiritually uplifted. I welcomed and treasured the friendship that these strangers displayed without restraint, shame, or guilt. It just didn't do my waistline or liver any good.

I chose to spend a few minutes each morning or evening doing some exercises in my hotel room. Half a dozen sets of thirty situps and thirty pushups created a reasonable illusion of physical fitness.

One night, I decided to venture into the local crowd and jog around the man-made lake. I estimated it to be approximately three miles, a decent distance to me. There was no pathway, no predetermined course to follow. I had to make my own trail, running partly in the streets, partly on the sidewalk, and occasionally on dirt paths leading into and between various buildings. I knew where I was, but felt lost. There was symbolism in there somewhere. I couldn't get my father out of my head.

I ran past apartments under construction, department stores teeming with humanity, small shops with single proprietors. The locals seemed to ignore me as I weaved my way among them.

I always prefer to run outdoors, in real places, without a preset pattern. Gyms and oval tracks are too regimented and repetitious. I like exploring and absorbing my surroundings, mixing with pedestrians, taking in small scenes from other people's daily lives.

I remember the cold wintry nights when I used to run through the Harvard campus and along the Charles River at midnight, revitalizing myself after a long evening of heavy studies or clearing my head after some cerebral or emotional exercise I put myself through on more than one occasion. The wind would whip at my face and the stars would twinkle through the stinging tears, mixing with my sweat. Of course, my asthma would kick up when I returned to my dorm and I would be left pacing the room, drenched in sweat, gasping for my life.

At camp, I used to run through the pine forest, weaving among the tall dry grass in a field of wild flowers. My nose would burn from the dust kicked up from the fallen leaves. At school, jogging on the fresh-cut grass meant spring was here and summer fast approaching and, along with that, my hay fever.

The thing about running outdoors is that it forces you to appreciate the mere fact of being alive. The senses get bombarded. Car fumes, Chinese food, Chanel perfume, sea breezes. The smells change from moment to moment. And you can't ignore them.

As I ran, I took in the sights. Huge mounds of green cabbage lined the roadside. Food kiosks spewed grease and clouds of steam, gathered bevies of hungry workers. Laborers shouldered huge loads of goods going from here to there and back. Life moves on here. No one stands still. No one has time to ponder the past or contemplate the future as I did.

As I rounded the far end of the lake, I took a left turn down a dirt path and happened upon a construction site. I was suddenly in a blind alley. Workers barely glanced at me and then resumed their menial tasks. I jogged in a circle a few times, peering between each unfinished building, finally realizing I was trapped in this dead end. I retreated back to the main street.

As I pulled away from the construction site, carefully picking my path back to the hotel, twisting my way through the sidewalk obstacle course, I suddenly experienced myself returning to my childhood days, squealing with unmitigated pleasure. It wasn't a specific place or sound. I didn't even see myself as the chubby boy I was then. It was just a feeling, a simple, unmistakable feeling of being "at home." Even as I was conscious of my thirty-eight-year-old body lumbering along the lakeside carrying ten, fifteen, or, God forbid, twenty extra pounds, awkwardly dodging groups of closely packed native Chinese, I felt thirty years of my life simply vanish.

There was absolutely nothing familiar about what I was doing or where I was in this foreign place on the "other side of the world." But the more I ran, the stronger and stronger this feeling kept getting. It was a feeling of something long gone, never again expected, and very pure. I sensed a clearing of all my emotions. A wiping clean of all worries, concerns, and pain. A cleansing of my body despite the dust swirling around me. The mental machinations, the surgical environment, the foreign experience all disintegrated into something safe and comforting.

I felt all of this in a split second. I didn't understand where it had originated from. But just like good love-making, I disengaged from the physicalness and mechanics of it and embraced the goodness and purity of the emotion.

I drew in one or two deep breaths, inhaling the sensation of "home." Then, it struck me. The memories and feelings of this purity from the past originated from a nearby pile of burning leaves. The dry, pungent smell of burning leaves, maple and oak perhaps, was something I hadn't smelled for decades.

Taking in a few more breaths, I slowed to nearly running-in-place. I was now at home in Quincy, raking in the freshly fallen leaves—dry, brown, crumbling—ripe for incineration. Jumping waist-high into the middle of the pile caused a rain of leaves to fall all around me. I was there, frolicking, as my father and uncle had frolicked in the fruit-filled orchard outside their modest home. Then, the fun having been spent, I rake the leaves into another neat pile by the side of the road. I can see my father watching me, perhaps with pride. He looks so young, his hair so dark and shiny. I light the pile and inhale the white smoke and sharp aroma of the burning leaves.

It surprised me to realize that the reason I was so startled by the ashy smell—at once so familiar and yet so strange—was not so much that I had smelled it as a child, but more that I *hadn't* smelled it for decades. It occurred to me that, just as the Communists in China had at one time outlawed Bible reading and Western medicine, environmental laws, inspired by the raising of consciousness in the 1960s, had outlawed the burning of leaves in my hometown. Too much pollution back East. Too much fire hazard out West. Burning leaves, which used to be a cultural ritual of Americana, was now a lost practice. That sensation was taken from me for nearly thirty years and might be lost entirely for the next generation.

In 1992, Los Angeles burned with the worst rioting in U.S. history. The smell of smoke that filled the skies was a vile and ugly odor. In the surgical suite, bone and flesh may burn. That smell is clinical and sterile. And there is a tragedy, as well as a humor, to burnt toast or charred turkey. No, the aroma of burning leaves is a unique, soulful, and happy experience, like that of freshly mowed grass or a crackling campfire. It is unforgettable.

I am the lucky one. Halfway around the world, in a land as foreign as there is, I am briefly reunited with home, and my life as a boy. The burning leaves give life to my memories.

A few paces beyond the smoldering pile I think, "This is my childhood I am breathing." And, as much as I may regret, it's my childhood I am running from, as fast as my overweight body can.

Though I wanted to stop and soak the fumes of these leaves into every pore and orifice of my body, to bathe in the innocence and simplicity of a distant past, the skies had quickly darkened. Night was fast approaching and I was running late for yet another festive banquet on my schedule.

As I headed back to my hotel, I wished my father were by my side, racing through the smoke, kicking at the drifting embers, coughing and choking with delight. I would have liked to hear him squeal with joy. I would have loved to see him sprint. I would have tried to match him stride for stride, even down a blind alley. But perhaps it was enough to share a smoky steamliner berth and hear him yell with glee at the threshold of his childhood home. It would have to be, since, being a good and obedient guest, I could not tarry in my dreams. For the Chinese were never late for an engagement—even if incurably drunk with the smell of life.

8

Eli's Secret

Yesterday was April 12, 1993, my oldest sister Mei-Mei's fortieth birthday. Ironic, isn't it, how we celebrate our relentless march toward the inevitable with a party. It's no wonder that surprise parties become more common as one grows older. Who really wants others to know how old we are? The only people celebrating with enthusiasm are the ones who aren't having a birthday. In fact, they're probably celebrating the fact that it *isn't* theirs.

It seems even more ironic that as we progress through more and more birthdays, the pull of the past gets stronger, and stronger as if our minds were like rubber bands, snapping back to a more familiar, tensionless state. We try to remember, if not relive, the past by rummaging through attics, writing nostalgic books, and throwing theme parties designed to embarrass each other. Mei-Mei's theme was the 1960s. Her friends were instructed to dress in groovy, hippie getups which, to me, looked strangely similar to the hip "grunge" look of the 1990s. Our brain must get totally confused on how to think and feel at occasions like this. We all know we've changed through the years, so we do things to reassure ourselves that things haven't, which only emphasizes the fact that it is *how* we perceive change that has changed, because even though *we* have, things really haven't. And that, in turn, will make us feel young—or old.

The birthday was the day before Easter and my brother-in-law, who had done all the planning, had asked everyone to arrive at seven o'clock. As we prepared for the arrival of the guests, my youngest sister (her birthday safely half a year away) and I reviewed the intricate process of coloring Easter eggs. We boiled the water in a large pot, dropped in the little fizzing tablet of dye, and spooned in some vinegar—just like we did as kids.

Using a wax pencil, we drew pictures of tulips and rabbits, spelled out the names of my nephews, and wrote offbeat, humorous phrases like "Mei-Mei's Last Egg" and "The Next Vogel" on the outer shells. I showed my sister how to spin the eggs on the counter top to see if they were hard-boiled. Raw eggs will flop unsteadily as if drunk, while hard-boiled eggs will spin tightly and stay erect. Of course, she already knew that.

We dipped the eggs into the small jars of dye, rotating them so as to color evenly using a thin wire hoop, the exact type we used half a lifetime ago. We were careful not to mix the dyes and even more careful to keep the eggs from cracking. We laughed at the seriousness with which we attacked the task to perfectly color these Easter eggs. Our reputation as creative and meticulous adult professionals—she, a pastry chef and I, a plastic surgeon—rested on it. Our pride as former children required it.

The guests began to arrive—long hair, bangles, beads and all. Many of them were strangers to me, but a few were friends I had known since high school. Most of them were married and many were also parents. Being neither at the time scared me. Had I missed the boat completely? One begins to doubt one's purpose in life.

When the women started probing me about plastic surgery, pointing out lines and wrinkles about their faces and eyes which, yes, I could actually see, I became even more scared. If they had aged to the point of thinking about plastic surgery, then I, too, must have aged. I, too, must look as if plastic surgery would do me some good. In actual fact, I knew it could. But I also knew too much to do it. There was nobody I trusted more than myself and I was too damn chicken.

Luckily, we got word that my brother-in-law was on his way over with my sister and her sons. That saved me from further self-doubts and fears of aging. Instead, we all ran around like the excited children we now were, strategically turning off lights to darken the room, but not so much that it looked suspicious.

"She'll see your shadow. Stand over here!"

"How will we know it's her and not your mother?"

"If we turn off all the lights in the kitchen, she'll get suspicious."

"Everyone shut up! Here she comes!"

Our ridiculous speculations ceased and we hid behind the banister leading to the second floor, positioning ourselves near the archway leading from the living room to the hallway entrance, through which she had to pass. We each jockeyed for position in the front.

They came in through the kitchen. We could hear the kids talking to their mom, trying to distract her. We stifled a collective giggle as the twins proved to be such good liars. A shadow appeared in the hallway. The lights came on and flashbulbs went off like firecrackers.

"Surprise!"

The flash caught my sister in a stunned expression. We laughed.

That's when the smallest guest, my youngest nephew, Eli, went berserk. It was as if a little bomb went off in the activity center of his two-and-a-half-year-old brain. He ran through the forest of adults, screaming with joy at the top of his lungs, waving his arms at nothing in the air, kicking wildly at the balloons we had strewn about the house. He seemed possessed with limitless happiness which could only explode in this frenzy of movement and noise. He looked like a little man out of control, bursting with an instinct to share his excitement with anyone he could smack into. The house roared with laughter at his frenetic antics and each adult lunged at him as if to harness for themselves some of that uninhibited energy and love of life.

Of course he neatly avoided our grasp. He knew something we didn't: perhaps that we adults would only stifle his joy and happiness and then he would spend the next forty years of his life trying to recapture it. When one of us was able to briefly catch him and hug him, he went into high-gear activity, kicking and screaming with discontent until we were forced to let him run loose again with reckless abandon, jumping up and down, clapping and flapping his hands like hummingbird wings. It was such a kick in the pants to watch.

As my sister went around the room in a much more systematic way, hugging and kissing her friends, the excitement began to die down and the conversation settled into typical reminiscing.

"And what have you been doing for the last fifteen years? . . . Oh, plastic surgery! That must be fascinating!"

"No, I haven't been back to the high school, have you?"

"I have three little ones. Do you have any? . . . Really? I thought you were married a *long, long* time ago!"

Eli had finally run out of gas and resumed his well-behaved demeanor, moving off to another room to play with his older brothers. As quickly as our childhood seemed to have passed, so did the child's play of the evening. Our cerebral cortex resumed control. The party for this milestone in my sister's life passed quietly into the night.

■　　■　　■

The next morning, Easter Sunday, Eli woke the household. He was an early riser and bounded about, ready for a new day, seeming to realize that grownups were slowing down his life. I love walks and, on this glorious spring morning, felt a particular need to take a stroll through the old neighborhood. Seeing Eli prancing around, waiting impatiently for the rest of the world to climb out of bed, made me yearn to see it through the eyes of a child. I thought about how hard it is to return to innocence.

Our perceptions change so quickly during our lifetime. Too often I feel I am not as conscious about things as I would like to be. Others have accused me of being too conscious, too introspective, too analytical. But it wasn't the analysis I was yearning for. That's the easiest part. It was the subconscious consciousness—like knowing that ice against the skin will sting and hurt but keeping the ice pressed firmly against the flesh. It's not to test your tolerance and induce masochistic pain, but to take the time and let your defenses go just enough to absorb the moment and the sensation fully—to feel exactly what cold ice pressed firmly against the flesh feels like. After a while, it's not cold at all.

I asked Eli if he wanted to go with me for a walk. Children at his age are more like pets than full-blown people. You expect them to do funny, irrational things in their own innocent way. They are often extensions of your own personality. Much of the time, it's hard to take them too seriously and that can be a dangerous posture. Often there is truth in innocence.

I used to ask the same thing of our French poodle, Elmo, who understood English and probably French and even Chinese. Elmo was a miniature reject from the toy poodle category. He would dart frantically around the room, not unlike the way Eli did the night before, barking and squealing, eager to be leashed up for a stroll around the neighborhood.

At that time, I never thought of looking at my neighborhood through Elmo's eyes. As it was, Elmo died when he ran away from home and got hit by a eighteen-wheel moving van. He was no match and we found him lying in the middle of the street a half mile from home. We buried him in our backyard, and my mother cried for a week.

Come to think of it, all of our pets had bad karma. Our first pets, five chickens we kept in a wire enclosure, ended up as chicken soup one evening. None of us kids wanted to eat this dish, although my father, practical guy that he is, gave it no second thought and feasted, having been the very one to take a chopping knife to their collective necks. I'm sure the soup tasted wonderful.

One of our pet rabbits ended up squashed to a pelt when my father accidentally ran it over. My father mistakenly thought this animal was smart enough to move from under the tires of our Lincoln Marquis. He discovered that rabbits aren't smart at all. Another rabbit contributed his body to science as an experimental animal in a family friend's laboratory. Neither Rob Franette nor Jack Frost had a chance. My sisters wouldn't talk to my father for a month.

All my goldfish ended belly-up from neglect, or perhaps poor oxygenation. My pet turtles disappeared from our outdoor fountain pool, victims of a roving neighborhood cat. My sister's Irish setter died of heat exhaustion in the family car one hot, humid summer day. I figured that with this history, animals within fifty feet of any of our family members should take heed and run, fly, or swim like hell the other way!

Eli hopped up and down excitedly like poor Elmo. He ran around in circles waiting for me to put on my shoes, forgetting to put on his own. He was so overwhelmed that when he tried to don his coat by a trick maneuver where he places it on the ground inside out and upside down, slips his arms through the sleeves and flips the coat over his head and down his back, this time he ended up with the coat upside down, the backside facing forward.

His coat corrected, we started down the street, the concrete sidewalk slippery with the morning sprinkle and the last of winter's breath in the cool air. We headed for the baseball diamond in the playground at the center of town. I had Eli hold my hand tightly. Actually it was just my little finger. He wasn't going to end up like Elmo if I could help it.

Birds were singing in the trees and I stopped to have him listen to their chirping. He pointed to them as they flew from branch to telephone pole and back again. His tracking system was a little too slow to keep up with their flitting about, but he was able to imitate their twittering sounds.

We crossed three streets before reaching the playground. Each time I taught him to look right, then left, then right again.

"Any cars, Eli?"

He dutifully looked right, then left, then right again, shaking his head.

"Okay, let's cross." Off we went, his chubby hand gripping my little finger as if he'd never let go.

We reached the playing field, deserted in the early morning solitude. The baseball diamond looked exactly as it had when I played on it as a Little Leaguer. It was here that I had earned the nickname King Kong, because I was twice the size of an average boy and in one glorious season swatted my way to a batting average over .700. The fences appeared so close now and the base path so small that I wondered how I hadn't hit 1.000. The bases themselves were missing but home plate was still firmly embedded in the ground.

I must have picked up a bat soon after putting down the feeding bottle. Although I can't remember precisely how I learned to play baseball, I do remember playing catch with my father. Knowing that my brother-in-law was not the athletic type, I took it upon myself, then and there, to teach Eli how to play baseball. I figured that a child's mind is like a sponge, soaking up all the impulses and impressions fed to it. While Eli may not recall this specific event and day in his life, perhaps enough of it would stick to his subconsciousness to appreciate it when he is half dead.

"Let's play baseball!"

I put Eli in the batter's box, planting his feet correctly so that he faced the pitcher's mound from the right-hand side. I stood ten feet away and threw him an imaginary pitch. "Here's the pitch. You hit it! What do you do?"

He looked at me expectantly. Or was it skeptically? How could I expect him to know something he's never seen?

"You run!"

And he ran after me to first base, squealing with excitement the whole way. He was safe.

"Okay, Eli. Here's another pitch. A hit again! What do you do?"

Again that quizzical look.

"You run!"

And we took off for second. Safe again.

"Another hit! Run!"

Safe at third.

"Another! Run!"

We peeled off down the third base line as fast as he could go. I was afraid he was going to trip and fall, his drive to reach home outstripping his ability to move his legs. But he didn't. He reached home and stood around looking at the plate, waiting for instructions. I was catching my breath wondering why he wasn't as tired as I was.

"What do you do now?"

I don't know why I half expected him to know. He looked up at me for directions one last time.

"Touch home plate."

So he squatted down and placed his tiny, fat palm firmly against the plate.

"You scored a run, Eli."

He laughed with joy. It seemed instinctual.

"Now you know how to play baseball." I realized that he had just scored the very first run in his very young life. He had made it safely all the way home.

As we left the baseball diamond, I doubted if he would remember the time his uncle ran the bases with him for the very first time. Even though his mind was a sponge, this was only make-believe today. I felt a little sad because I had so much to teach him that he wouldn't ever remember.

We walked finger in hand toward the swings. The early spring grass was moist with the previous evening's rainfall and large puddles had formed in the various low spots of the playground. As we carefully picked our way through the field, I noticed a crinkling sound in the air. It was very still and we were all alone in this vast playground. I looked around and heard the sound again. I'd never heard this sound before. Wherever we turned, we heard it. It seemed to be surrounding us and, at the same time, right under us. It was almost as if it were coming from right within ourselves.

"Eli. Listen. What's that?"

He stopped.

"Listen. What do you hear?"

A rustling sound. Like plastic wrapping being squished between the fingers. Crinkle. Crinkle. All around us.

"It's the grass."

He stooped close to the ground as I lowered my ear to the wet field. He mimicked me and bent over completely. I'd never noticed this sound before, but it had to have always been there.

"The grass is talking to you."

He stood quietly, mesmerized by the sound. A tiny, fragile human being, soaking up all the life of the world as it bombarded his senses. He was trying to hear the words of the rainwater percolating through the fresh grass and soil.

"Hear what it's saying?"

He listened motionlessly.

"It's a secret."

He bent down, collapsing his body until his ear touched the tips of the blades. I only wished I could bend so low. He struggled to hear exactly what his uncle was hearing.

"It's saying 'I love you.' It's the grass talking to you, Eli."

He seemed struck by that and didn't say a word, trying to understand what that meant to have the grass tell him secrets. It was probably too metaphorical for his young mind.

We continued on, playing on the swings and slides, and then, our fun spent, walked to the town's drugstore two blocks away to look for an Easter card for his Grandma and Grandpa, my parents. He rejected six before he settled on a simple one with two adult rabbits hugging a baby rabbit. I helped him sign the card with his name and we started back home, coming across my father's car outside our neighborhood church. We put the card on the windshield so that my father and mother would see it when they came out from church. Then we went inside and sat down in the last row of pews in the back. The bellringers were playing an Easter song, so I pointed them out to Eli, who watched with quiet fascination. He didn't move throughout the entire song. I wished I knew what was going through his mind.

Prayers began and Eli soon fell asleep in the pew. He slept through the entire service as I daydreamed about my life today, the way I usually did as a teenager, thinking about everything but the service. I don't know if other people do this, but I often use one activity as a diversion to contemplate another. When exercising, I think about writing. When writing, I think about meditating. When meditating, I think about playing music. When playing music, I think about sports. When playing sports, I think about, well, playing other sports.

Sitting in the pew, among the familiar pillars and stained glass window scenes from the Bible, I thought about the pain and suffering of so many people in the world. I thought about my days as an altar boy, now rarely going to service except for Christmas and Easter. I thought about the times I used to play the violin in church, though now I only beat the rust from my fingers every six to twelve months. I thought about my family's ironic and diverse living situations: my parents tolerating each other into their fifth decade together; my younger sister now separated, headed for divorce after five years of marriage; my older sister happily married with three great sons; and me, once a confirmed bachelor, still single, contemplating my upcoming marriage. I thought about my aging body, my stunted emotions, my inflated expectations and fading dreams. I thought about people I grew up with and whom I see once every decade, or will never see again. I thought about my future, whether my future was to be my present, or was already in my past. I thought too much.

That life is fleeting is a cliché and yet it stands so still. The mind gets out in front of the body as much and as often as the body precedes the mind. Rarely are they synchronized, except at birth and in death. When they're not, they often get in each other's way. An aging body impedes a youthful mind, and a declining mind handicaps a vibrant body.

My fortieth birthday is just over a year away. I'm glad for my sister that it's behind her although she seemed to handle it well. That hurdle will not be easy for me. Reaching thirty was difficult. The disappointment will come not only with the disappointments themselves and the realization of my limitations, but also with the acceptance of them. Everything seems futile when you need to struggle so hard and reach so deep to pull those experiences from the past, experiences that seemed routine and insignificant, but now have become so precious as memories. The home run trot around the bases. The coloring of Easter eggs. The acid rock music of the 1960s. One easily forgets.

After the service, I walked back home with Eli. He seemed to grip my little finger even tighter. He didn't say much. Maybe it was because he was still groggy from sleep. Or maybe, he, too, was contemplating life. He pointed to the sparrows chirping in the trees. We looked to the right, then the left, then right again before we crossed the last street. Then we ran a race home.

When we finally reached home—Eli just two steps ahead of me—I felt very close to Eli. I enjoyed our solitary time together. It was my chance to play dad a little, although the usual advantage of being an uncle is that you can relinquish your role of dad at any time. Soon I would return to that role of being just uncle, say my goodbyes to Eli and his brothers, and return to my home three thousand miles away, pretending I didn't miss the last twenty-five years away from home and family; knowing that this very special day for me would be lost among so many other days in Eli's short life; knowing he will forget our time together and one day will take a walk with someone half a lifetime into the future, racking his heart and brain to remember the valuable experiences in his life and how he learned to play baseball. That is life.

My sister was waiting for us when we returned. The two of them hugged.

"What did you do, Eli?"

I was sure he wouldn't remember.

"We played baseball."

"You played baseball?" My sister looked at me puzzled.

"We pretended," I explained. "Make-believe." I half wished it wasn't so. "What do you do when you hit the ball, Eli?"

He thought for a moment. He'd forgotten.

"Run."

I was amazed. "Right! You run!" I had to test him further. "What else did we do?"

"Listen to the grass."

My sister was confused. But I was full of joy.

"What sound does the grass make?" I explained our discovery of the talking grass as Eli blew soft crinkling sounds through his lips.

"And what did the grass say to you?"

I held my breath as if it were going to be my last.

"It said 'I love you.' "

He giggled. So happy-go-lucky.

"Yes." I said quietly. I slowly let my breath out.

"I love you."

9

Ten Thousand Dead Ants

I often walked with my head hanging down during my childhood, staring at the ground, not out of shame or embarrassment, but because I was a gentle and careful boy. I was always wary of that pile of dog doo and also had an undying concern for my mother's back. And if I wasn't avoiding the crack that'd break my mother's back, it was that lonesome ant wandering across my path.

Most people, kids especially, cared less about stepping on a solitary ant. Ants were everywhere. They seemed dispensable. Catching a bus, chasing an itinerant ball, or just getting from point A to point B was infinitely more important than the life of an ant. In fact, much of a boy's time was spent seeking out various insects to torture and destroy. Crucifying butterflies, skewering and dividing earthworms, and smashing flies against a freshly washed car window were all legitimate sporting events.

Even the ants themselves were targets. Once a boy learned how to burn a dried oak leaf using a magnifying glass, moving objects became the next obligatory challenge and ants were perfect: they were small enough to test accuracy and slow enough to demand steadiness. Ants definitely helped my friends develop hand-eye coordination. Some ants were spared, only to unwittingly lead my friends to their ant homes. Many an anthill was leveled or plugged with grains of sand. Yet ants, at least as a group, were seemingly indestructible. They were dumb, unrelenting survivors. Ants freshly interned within a sandy tomb soon emerged unscathed and unperturbed to carry on with their labors. New anthills and new trails popped up like dandelions in spring. Ants were forever. Perhaps that is why no one felt guilty about the dastardly deeds of destruction inflicted upon these innocent ants. No one, that is, but me.

I personally never intentionally killed an ant in my boyhood days. The sight of an ant in my path was a signal for me to change my course in order to avoid the creature. As silly as it sounds, that is the absolute truth. While it might have been a symptom of being a sissy, I like to think that I believed that ants, no matter how meager and insignificant, were also one of God's treasured creations. I certainly had that general concept incorporated in my early learning environment as a Christian singing "Jesus Loves the Little Children" and repeating the story of the Creation and Noah's Ark, although ants themselves were never specifically mentioned. Oh, the innocence of youth!

Why I carried this belief to such an extreme as to protect ants is somewhat of a mystery since none of my friends, no matter how supersissy or overly religious, seemed to care much about stepping on an ant. They probably never gave it much thought. And when the time called for it, even my father didn't mind beheading pet chickens for dinner or gutting fish still gasping for air and flopping around on deck. And he is one of the most gentle, caring, and religious men I know.

I'd like to think that humankind's basic instinct is one of Rousseau-like purity. Infants are not hateful or destructive by nature. Most just want to lie around; stare off into space; and get fed, hugged, and left alone to grow—but not into mean, hateful, vengeful, warmongering adults. They'll blink at a hovering bee, cry at a fly in their ear, and squirm when ants crawl on their smooth, soft flesh. But they won't deliberately seek to torture or demolish the many other ranks of living creatures. That is something they learn to do later on in life—as older kids and especially as grownups.

The same is basically true of animals. Poisonous animals are not innately cruel. Aggressive animals do not kill for pleasure. Most animals are just trying to get along and survive. Except for ants, as I'd find out one day.

■   ■   ■

I must admit that one of the instincts I had was to identify emotionally with things and people besides myself—a sort of "walk in another's shoes" type of mentality. That really isn't a bad habit to have. It's what we teach our kids.

Storytelling is basically an attempt at getting the audience to identify with the subject. Kafka used an insect in his *Metamorphosis* and Barth used a sperm in *Night-Sea Journey*. The more you can effect the identification, the easier your task of persuasion.

This sensitivity led me to consider the sensation of being crushed to death by the monstrous shoe of a fat Chinese kid. That mental image convinced me that preventing the same condition in any animal, including an ant, was worthy of my meager efforts. At my age I couldn't imagine what it really would be like if whole populations of fat Chinese kids were splattered across the asphalt streets of my neighborhood, carelessly flattened by the sticky pads of a humongous mutant ant. It probably wouldn't be a pretty sight.

So I continued to keep my head tilted down to the ground in search of that unsuspecting ant that might unfortunately wander into my path. As I grew more preoccupied with the real—and bigger—aspects of life (like filling my brain with knowledge and my address book with women's phone numbers), my eyes became more fixed on the horizon—where I was going and what was around me—and not so much on what was under me.

Ants hardly entered my mind.

I'm positive I've stepped on hundreds of them throughout my adult life. I apologize to those who met the soles of my feet. I do know that a quick death is merciful and to be an injured ant is worse than being a dead one. There are no ant hospitals or ant paramedics, although ants will carry other ants away. I don't know if it is instinctive, ritualistic, or just another of life's physical burdens that ants seem to relish like hauling trillions of grains of sand and dirt from one place to another in their busy, busy life. A dead ant on another ant's shoulder may be as good as a granule of granite to the domineering queen ant.

At any rate, the ants I observed to be injured were promptly and mercifully put out of their misery as a gesture of human efficiency and kindness, not destructiveness. Most of the time I didn't even know they were actually suffering. And to be honest, I didn't care. At least not as much as I did when I was a little boy. Occasionally, usually as a group, they became temporary nuisances—at a beach picnic or outdoor barbecue where they were matter-of-factly swept harmlessly and painlessly away—cursed, but not harmed. Their being a nuisance ended when we packed up our food and playthings and left their home to return to ours.

Years, even decades, have passed since those days of caring for ants. I have led a relatively productive life learning the craft of plastic surgery, helping the injured and deformed, enhancing the imperfect, and perhaps saving a life or two along the way. I have never been in a physical altercation since junior high school unless you count the half-playful, half-serious boxing and wrestling matches my wife, Joanne, and I used to have over things like engagement and marriage and who did more housework. I've never shot a deer, skinned a snake, speared a fish, or broken the neck of a chicken—unless it was already barbecued. I've never fired a weapon, gone to war, or been personally involved in a riot. I've never even cursed or threatened another human being, and still think that all things living on earth are God's blessed creation. I don't believe in waste, acts of malice, or games of torture.

Yet lately, I've begun to lower my head again, looking for ants, hunting them down. I feel unnervingly agitated when I see one and can hardly contain myself when I see two. You see, ants have become my enemy.

■　　■　　■

It started just a month or two ago. I happened to see an ant in my otherwise spotless house. It wasn't a killer red ant, Australian bulldog, Amazon, or kamikazi mutant. It was a regular household variety black ant. So I probably overreacted a bit when I yelled with exceeding alarm, "There's an ant in the house!"

Joanne, good-natured person that she is, laughed at me. "You've never seen an ant before? A grown man so afraid of bugs! You're silly!"

Silly indeed.

You see, Joanne is from the central mountainous part of the island of Jamaica. Bush country as she calls it. And she is, in many respects, truly a country bumpkin. She herself will readily admit it. She grew up with bugs all around and is unfazed by the sight of creepy, crawly things. Certainly not an ant!

I was rather irritated by her insensitive assessment of the situation because my urban and urbane intellect knew better than she: where there's one ant, there's another. And where there are two, there's trouble. Ants don't come alone. They come in armies. "The ants are marching two by two, hurrah, hurrah. . . ."

This particular ant got off easy. I swallowed my pride and instincts of superiority and omniscience, picking up the ant between my thumb and forefinger so as not to squish it. Not a simple task with an insect as small as an ant. With Joanne still laughing at me in the background and visions of a giant shoe hovering over my head, I tossed the intruder out the third-floor window, knowing full well that, with such a small body and light weight, the ant would reach terminal velocity long before it landed on the hillside some fifty to sixty feet below with hardly a bruise on its precious torso.

But I was worried. And rightly so.

The ants did come. First in single file, then by columns, in less than an evening. They swarmed over the kitchen counter and invaded the master bedroom. They trailed from a ventilation duct into the living room, across the threshold of our dining room and around one wall of the kitchen to end up in the laundry room. They tracked from the sidewalk, up the short, stone-paved driveway, and into the garage to feast on the garbage left in bags between our two cars. They were everywhere.

As soon as I swept them away, they were back. I washed the counter tops and sealed up all the food that seemed to attract them. But they always discovered that one miniscule drop of gravy or jam which lay innocently on the tiled floor or granite counter. They were unrelenting and frightening. I knew from childhood that they were virtually invincible as a group.

The broom proved to be of no avail. I progressed to a wash rag when Joanne told me how they follow the chemical trail left by their sticky little feet. I ended up with a turbocharged Hoover vacuum cleaner which I hauled throughout my eight-room house, sucking up all the patrolling scouts. Joanne continued to be amused by all of this—the sight of a grown man, armed with two degrees from Harvard and a Hoover vacuum cleaner, hunting ants in his own house.

But they just kept coming. I could see them as they wound their way through and around, in and out of the house. Their trail was like a living organism that wouldn't die. It pulsated. It seethed. As soon as I swept one group away, another battalion marched in to be sucked up by the Hoover. They had no fear of death. This uneven battle with these multiple skirmishes went on for weeks. With such a multi-pronged incursion, I felt I was not about to find a solitary mother nest. Ant bait and traps were ineffective. The ants were slowly but surely wearing me down. I was becoming frustrated and indignant.

It was then that I came across the most frightening scene of all. We have a maid's room off the kitchen. Since we don't have a live-in maid, the room is never used. While investigating a well-populated trail winding its way from an outside staircase into the maid's room, I found it entering into the adjacent, sealed-off bathroom. I opened the door and gagged, a chill running up my neck.

Our maid's bathroom had literally been overrun with ants. Thousand and thousands of ants piled hundreds deep in three or four mounds on the floor around the toilet. The black mounds, measuring many inches high, took on a morbid and sinister quality, as if the ants were staking out a claim to this room and, thus, to my whole house. It was as if I had found a morgue of invaders, suffocated by their own uncontrollable replication, their dead numbers mute testimony to their determination for conquest and their willingness to sacrifice all they had.

I realized I had discovered a secret breeding ground for one group of these ants. Who knows how long they had been there, plotting their *coup d'état*? Who knows how many other undiscovered encampments lay hidden within my house? Could they be lurking in the dark corners of my closet or lying in wait under my bed or planting their armies in my shoes? Would I soon uncover a swarm of ants feasting in a jar of boysenberry jam or playing in my box of raisin bran?

It was then that I had had enough. No more Mister Nice Guy! No more gentility! I was through looking down at my feet to see if another ant or two had entered my abode. I felt violated, assaulted. I wanted them out, vanquished, gone for good.

So while keeping my head down in search of wandering ants reminded me of my childhood days and imbued me with guilt, I did something I would never have done half a lifetime ago. I slaughtered ants by the tens of thousands.

Not being content with merely sucking them into the Hoover along with various other insects and arthropods, I proceeded to asphyxiate their armies with an ant-killing chemical chaser, creating my own ant gas chamber. Not satisfied with that modality, I fumigated them with an industrial-strength insecticide. And when the opportunity presented itself I drowned them in the toilet, in the shower, and with the garden hose.

Now and then, I wouldn't be at all timid and actually crushed them with my fingers or even my bare feet. After the first few difficult kills, it became thoughtless child's play. Eradicate at whatever cost! Kill or be killed!

As it became clear that even with this vicious degree of assault they were still dominating the house, I finally gave in to Joanne (who by this time was even more angry and intolerant than I). In came the professional ant buster to spray the whole property with pesticide. In those two hours of spraying, millions of ants (beyond the tens of thousands for whom I proudly and unrepentantly take credit and responsibility) met their demise. Bodies writhed like Mexican jumping beans for a second or two, then lay still forever. Tiny black corpses lay strewn throughout the house. And the residue of pesticide continued its effective work for weeks thereafter.

Well, that did the trick! Since then, we haven't seen a solitary ant in the house. We now spray every three months. Soon, we went back to our sleeping and eating without the threat of intruders. Life was peaceful and wonderful again.

■   ■   ■

The triumph, however, is a victory with a price, as is true of all victories. The price is the realization that such a small thing in life as ants can change me, and that tolerance is relative. Despite my sensitivity and perceived niceness as a human being and my respect for all living things, I have my limits, which end at the loss of my freedom and the need to survive.

All this took me by surprise. Even as Joanne and I laughed at the silliness of my guilt, as well as pride, at slaying tens of thousands of ants, I was well aware of the feeling of loss, not so much of the loss of life, but of my innocence, which I had protected and believed in for so many decades. The hanging down of my head to watch out for and protect the ants had turned into the hanging down of my head in order to destroy them. Although it sounds ridiculous to extrapolate, I wondered what it would take to go from ants to humans. If tested, how far could I go?

For this brief moment, halfway into my life, I was able to take a glimpse into the mind of destruction—my mind—and understand how fine the line is between ants and humans, tolerance and survival, good and evil. There is a wistful hope that I will pass from this earth before I need to cross that fine line again. That next time might be too easy. And I do not hate ants.

Yet in the end, along with a sense of regret, there is an ironic sense of relief, to know myself, my imperfections, and my suppressed capacity for destruction. To see the world in another's shoes. And to realize that that other shoe may be my own. There is some redemption in that self-revelatory image. For that, ten thousand ants did not die in vain.

10

The Big Bang

Consider this question: What causes the sober, cynical, despairing condition of man as one crosses the halfway point of life, the so-called *mid-life crisis* in all its forms?

I have the answer. It's not that we are fat or haven't accomplished anything. It has nothing to do with our wives who don't understand us, or being husbands who don't attend to them, or the lack of any spouse. It has less to do with where we are than where we have been and where we are going.

It is so obvious once one takes a minute or two to think about it. The only reason the answer has been elusive for so long is that the explanation is linked to the origin of the universe, and thus of humankind as a whole, instead of *individual* men or women. Furthermore, it is something that is evident predominantly by virtue of its absence rather than its presence. Sound confusing? It isn't. It's the Big Bang.

The Big Bang theory has been advanced by astronomers and astrophysicists as a cataclysmic explosion whereby the universe and all of its physical components were created and through which the universe becomes infinitely expansive. The reverse of this event is the enigmatic black hole. And while the Big Bang is the ultimate cosmic awakening that continues to drive life as we know it even today, the physical properties of a black hole are constantly being challenged and revised. The idea that particles cannot escape from the eternal trap of the sucking black hole was disproved by that curious but brilliant scientist Stephen Hawking. He revealed that the Heisenberg uncertainty principle of quantum mechanics explains how virtual particles can fragment and lose their partner which, holding true to the second law of thermodynamics and the theory of increasing entropy, causes an expected radiation to emanate from the black hole. Thus, black holes are merely real dark gray splotches. Despite these theoretical vacillations, the unifying analogy of astrological phenomena and the human emotional condition is still quite viable. Things *can* escape a black hole: things such as hope.

As I sit and analyze the root of my own small personal agonies (which have been agonizing only because of all my analyzing) throughout my blessed life and, in particular, the reason why so many civilized human beings fall into that black hole of mid-life despair, I realize that the big bangs of life, as opposed to astronomy, are neither all that big nor always such a bang. This doesn't mean that they don't exist; they're just less easily appreciated.

Throughout most of childhood, there are relative big bangs that keep us going (just as there are relative black holes that keep us sober). They are the gold stars, the ice cream treats, the acceptance by peers and the new friends, all of which produce a continuum of big bangs. Certainly the progression through one grade after the other and the receiving of diplomas, ribbons, and cash rewards for all the As are little big bangs that are built into the system of growing up. When one fails to progress or graduate or integrate socially, the bang fizzles and despair sets in. Thus appear the black holes of childhood and adolescence.

The Big Bang theory is definitely appropriate in more ways than one when one looks at social interaction between the sexes. Both sexes expect their own version of a big bang when relationships start to develop. I certainly do when my animal juices start to flow. Imagine the theory applied literally to the dating scene, when two humans begin an intimate interplay. At first, movements are slow and deliberate. Temperatures begin at comfortable life-sustaining levels. As movement increases, mind and body entangle and temperatures rise through various boiling points. An ever-accelerating chemical reaction occurs. One loses all control.

Bang! . . . Life can change in a hurry.

On the other hand, consider the rapid deflation of egos when the bang is only a little pop. We've all been there. Many scorned suitors and discarded damsels have filled the galaxies of life with a myriad of black holes.

When one gets used to all the big bangs, one is understandably disturbed when life gets too quiet. And that is precisely what happens when discontent sets in: the discontent of mid-life. It sneaks up on us because the explosions of childhood are so far removed from our present travels as adults. We hardly ever notice the absence of sound.

■   ■   ■

The first time the silence really bothered me was during my surgical residency. I was about twenty-five, a couple of years into my postgraduate training and newly transferred into a young general surgical program in Los Angeles. I had been prepped and revved up by a high-powered medical school curriculum and an environment of unparalleled intensity at Harvard Medical School and now found myself understimulated in my new environment. I expected so much and remembered the saying about there being two types of learning institutions: Harvard—and all the rest. Because the training program was in a predominately private-practice hospital, residents had very few of their own cases and very little responsibility or autonomy. Work was still long and hard, but self-satisfaction and challenges were few and far between. I remember thinking, "Is this all it is? Am I wasting my time, mind, and energy waiting for an opportunity to stretch itself out on an operating room table?"

So, I did something that was unheard-of at that time in surgical training. I bailed out. There seemed to be no bang at the time, so I went in search of it.

For two years, I wrote screenplays, played music, and taught tennis. I hung out with dreamers in the film industry. I spent time at laundromats, coffee shops, and bus stops where all of humanity collides. I traveled. I wandered. I played Bach partitas, Mozart concertos, and Beethoven sonatas for hours. I took long walks on the beach in Santa Monica and spent long hours with friends watching wave after wave crash against stone pilings while discussing the meaning of life and why men and women are hopelessly at odds with each other. I chased women as much as ran from them. I did butt thrusts and leg lifts with innumerable celebrities at Jane Fonda's Workout. I watched so many reruns of "Bonanza," all with happy endings, that I almost believed I was a fourth Cartwright son on the Ponderosa.

I sold no scripts, gave no concerts, and could barely buy groceries or tennis balls on my teaching fees, but I soon came to realize that the search itself was a big bang. Big bangs had to do with change. They had to do with acceleration and a sense of movement. They required forward progress and an expansion of life. After these two years passed, feeling terrifically satisfied about my hiatus from medicine, I proselytized to younger medical students and residents about the need to feel unfeigned enthusiasm for one's profession or life situation, or get the hell out.

It is inevitable that anyone with such a love for a profession as I feel for medicine and plastic surgery may discover that everything will someday never be enough. At the risk of sounding ungrateful, something will always be missing and the rest of your life will be spent in restless despair or in constant search of that elusive "something." I am well into my private practice as a plastic surgeon at one of the world's most prestigious medical centers located in one of the world's most celebrated plastic surgery watering holes. My whole life has been spent preparing (even though, at times, subconsciously) for what should be the biggest bang of my life.

■　　■　　■

I began my formal education at the ripe old age of two and a half because I was bored at home while my older sister and lots of other children were learning things at school that I had yet to understand, but wanted to. In kindergarten I learned math while the other kids played with blocks. I proceeded to skip first grade, and a few years later I skipped my first year at Harvard. I crammed four years of higher learning into three, taking up to six courses in one semester. Upon graduating, in my hell-bent drive toward adulthood, I went straight to Harvard Medical School during an era when most students were looking for ways to delay entry into the "real" world. I graduated at twenty-three and began my surgical training in my first choice of institutions. I finished training at some of the best medical centers in all the world. And now I hope I've earned the respect of plastic surgery's toughest community in Beverly Hills.

It should be like the spelling bee, where once you have spelled all the words thrown at you, you get a trophy. Or if you finish all the food on your plate, you get dessert. Or if you feed a girl, treat her right, and show her a good time, you get a big bang. Right? Wrong! It is a myth. What really happens is that the trophy is just a puny little ribbon and you are eliminated for spelling "recompense" instead of "recompensed." You eat until you vomit. And the girl gives you a big bang, but a year later you can't remember each other's name. It's the spelling bee itself, the act of feeding, and the courtship dance alone which are the bangs of life. Being in the very place I'm in should be part of the big bang itself.

While I did not consciously set goals for myself when I set upon the path of medicine, I'm sure there was a subtle infusion of expectations that developed. I certainly know of some colleagues who set definite goals for themselves: e.g., living in a million-dollar house in Bel Air (now worth perhaps seven hundred and fifty thousand dollars if they're lucky) or being the plastic surgeon to the stars (which, unfortunately, only ninety-nine out of the hundred or so plastic surgeons in the Beverly Hills area can, or will, claim to be). Others have more modest goals like having two kids or only one wife or a cabin overlooking Lake Arrowhead. I never thought too much about such goals. My view of life is that of an infinitely tall mountain that one sets out to climb. One cannot see the top or know how far one is from the summit, nor even if the summit exists. One may not remember the base. One can only see the few surrounding feet of mountainside. There may be multiple paths to take or even no obvious path at all. But the most important thing to do is to always be sure one is going up.

It is an ironic coincidence that I live in a house perched on a ridge high above Beverly Hills, just short of an ill-defined peak before the road dead-ends and for which there are no signs. The main street leading up to my house, which is winding and narrow with multiple hairpin turns, has a dozen or so side streets, each of which trails off the mountain into some nearby canyon. Whenever I instruct friends on how to reach my house, I tell them to keep heading uphill and if they feel themselves going downhill, they're going the wrong way. No one has failed to find my house even if it means driving at a snail's pace for fear of ending up in a canyon ditch. Such is life.

One interesting fact about climbing this proverbial mountain of life is that the going is hard at the beginning but we soon are encouraged by the exhilaration of our journey and the freshness of our energy. Each foot of progress is immediately evident as the ground falls away during the climb. As the climb progresses farther from the ground, the results seem less dramatic as measured against the perceived change in our environment. The reality is that the journey gets easier because the pull of gravity rapidly diminishes, if only we can keep up our energy and enthusiasm. Eventually, the effort required for this journey approaches zero as the climb proceeds infinitely far from the ground and progress occurs infinitely fast. Unfortunately, the perception of movement is also minimal and approaches zero. One must begin to appreciate the panorama.

So, while I didn't always have clear-cut points of destination, there was always an awareness of direction and progression, and a speed of progression. It is the speed of progression, or rather the increase in acceleration, that separates an expansion from a big bang. And just as in the sensation of landing in an airplane, the feeling of slowing down negates the fact that you are still traveling faster than you could ever dream, sitting securely in a seat with your seatbelt fastened and your chairback and tray table in a fully upright and locked position.

■　■　■

There is a dilemma. Undoubtedly most people who know me envy me, even if just a little bit. As such, they cannot be sympathetic to the discontent in someone who has achieved what appears on the surface to be goals that most men would have set and accepted for themselves. Intellectually and rationally I know and understand this. Emotionally it is an entirely different matter. I practice an incredibly diverse type of plastic surgery. My practice is rare in this era of super-specialization, but I feel it is vital to the field, especially for purists. Plastic surgery is not a profession of procedures or techniques as most people assume (the procedures and techniques soon become obsolete as fads, but continue as tools). Rather, it is an artistic discipline of thought and application. It's anatomic problem solving. In its purist form, it involves customized solutions to surgical, as well as perceptual, problems. I could always ask for more patients but couldn't ask for more purity. That is an accomplishment of which I am very proud. Yet there is still the specter of dissatisfaction.

Medicine in the 1990s is going through some horrific growing pains in a real and literal sense. It is expanding so fast as to become a big bang itself, threatening everything around it. But the solutions proposed may be the equivalent of black holes into which medicine and everything else will be sucked. One should be cautious of the admonition, "Be careful of what you wish for. You just might get it." And you'll lose your soul for it.

The mechanism to move the bias in medicine toward "less for more" may in the end lead us directly to "little for all." The main relevance to my mid-life condition is that the number of big bangs has diminished noticeably. Big bangs in medicine today on an individual level are elusive, as various forms of constraints make "health care providers" feel more and more like indentured servants rather than valued professionals. And along the way, the spirit of medicine is trampled, its soul sucked dry, and patients become a mere commodity for the transfer of cash. With a multitude of big bangs in my past, I begin to wonder where and when the next will occur. I wonder where all the sound has gone.

Gang-bangers in the inner city, on the other hand, often have few, if any, big bangs early in life such as getting jobs or graduating from high school. But like all humans they still crave the bang and strive to create some for themselves. Unfortunately, too many of them create big bangs called drive-by shootings and drug dealing. They find out too late that their big bangs are really black holes and their explosion are more like implosions. I, in contrast, rarely sought to create big bangs, but was frequently blessed by their presence. So now, in their absence, like so many around me in their own small way, I find myself orbiting the black holes of mid-life, feeling more and more like the airplane is about to land—in a big, black, empty hole.

I know most people reading this are starting to feel their own black hole calling them closer because the mood seems so morose and the writing so pessimistic. Let me assure you that that is not my intent. One's natural reaction is to go in search of big bangs. Thus follows the academic sabbatical, the engineer now celestial navigator, the doctor turned writer. Or, less optimistically, one surrenders to the pull of the black holes. Thus, the molesting clergyman, the Romeo now weeping Cyrano, the homeless former millionaire. Whole industries and professions are built on big bangs and black holes. And for some, it is more important to continue the procession of big bangs, while for others, it is the need to avoid the black holes.

Besides the time I bailed out from medicine, I have been lucky to have avoided the dreaded black holes of life. I have certainly felt their gravity, such as the time I planned to travel over six thousand miles from Los Angeles to London to rendezvous with a promising big bang, a smashing, mature woman-child of eighteen, only to have her literally disappear into the arms of another man, who, in all probability, was destroyed by the resultant explosion (and rightly and deservedly so). Instead of vanishing into the impending black hole of loneliness, despondency, and self-pity, I chose to use its gravitational pull, traveling undaunted to England, and then blasting through the other side of the black hole toward Paris, having the best time of my life—alone, unconstrained—exploring the richness of English theater and Parisian art. Your mind need never be alone.

Then there was the time I was in my athletic prime (my early thirties if I remember), skiing the freshly powdered slopes of Snowbird in Utah, when I promptly threw out my back during a sneezing fit while performing the prodigious athletic feat of climbing out of bed. Not only did I lose three days of glorious new snow, but I realized that I no longer could afford to sneeze with such reckless abandon. Though never the daredevil, I still felt the blow of this revelation. To this day, I sneeze with my mouth wide open and cajole my one hundred-fifteen-pound wife into carrying all my luggage and skis.

So you can see, my black holes have been few and relatively insignificant. My main realization in life has been in experiencing the big bangs that come my way, not in dodging oncoming black holes. I suspect that this is the case with most people.

So the question now posed is what the hell do astronomy and cosmic mechanisms have to do with cerebral machinations and the stage of being half dead? Part of the answer came a few days ago when my mother called to say that Mr. Flaherty, who had been our next-door neighbor in Quincy, passed away from a brain tumor. This was one of life's cynical ironies, since Mr. Flaherty's next-door neighbor for more than ten years was none other than my father, the famous brain surgeon.

Mr. Flaherty wasn't just another next-door neighbor. In fact, he embodied everything good about life when I was a kid. He was the jovial father of my best friend, Eddie, who always stuck up for me and protected me around the neighborhood. He was the son of Grampy, my beloved surrogate grandfather, who taught me everything about keeping score for the Boston Red Sox. Never once in my whole, half-spent life had I seen Mr. Flaherty yell or scream, except when Ted Williams hit a home run. Never did he appear sad or dejected, except when we moved from the neighborhood. Even then, he was able to offer hearty good wishes for our happiness and prosperity. He was someone very special whom I admittedly took for granted, as many of us do so many others. Death is the ultimate and only black hole from which there is no current earthly escape. As such, all other black holes we encounter in life are dwarfed in significance, no matter how strongly we feel their pull, no matter how deep and dark. Escape, however difficult and inexorably slow, is always forthcoming.

The real key to life, then, lies in actively maximizing big bangs throughout the span of one's life and accepting the belief that the biggest bang occurred at birth, the blackest hole will come in death, and the only thing we can even hope to control is what comes in between. It's not religion and it's not philosophy. It's not astronomy and it's not really science. It's just the unarguable truth.

The true Big Bang is something that continues forever and ever, like the ever-expanding universe. It is irreversible to the extent that the universe is not ever expected to collapse to nothingness and it will never cease to be relevant. So it is that my birth set into perpetual motion a thing called my life. It, too, is expanding toward the summit, toward infinity. It will come to end in some distant day but never ever collapse into nothingness. And hurtling through time and space, I will often not appreciate how wonderfully fast I am traveling on the crest of this, the biggest bang of all.

11

Forever and Ever

This evening, I contemplated forever. Or rather, to be more exact, I contemplated the concept of forever. It's something I do frequently, in pieces, for finite bits of time, to drive myself crazy. But also to appreciate life just a little more.

Earlier, at dusk, I was out for my triweekly, sometimes trimonthly, jog—three laps up and down a half-mile hill right outside my house. There is a gradual upward slope for the first third, a plateau for the middle third, followed by a steep, unrelenting thirty-degree rise to the top. This road is at the very top of a ridge with spectacular views of the lush canyon below and the dazzling city skyline off in the distance. On a clear day, you can even see sailboats dotting the blue ocean, their white sails floating as if suspended from the clouds like decorative mobiles. There are wildflowers and native bushes growing on the falling slope and it seems you are on the top of your own private world. The jogs usually kill me: physically because of the incline, mentally because of the repetition. Jogging is one thing I can't do forever.

I managed to plod through the first two laps today, looking forward to the peak each time since I knew it meant an exhilarating four minutes of running straight downhill. At the same time, I dreaded the final few feet at the bottom of the course since then I had only to anticipate another six agonizing minutes of uphill climb. The final lap blew out my brain as I concentrated hard on blocking out the pain of the uphill struggle. I could feel each cortical vessel throb. My thighs and buttocks burned. Puffing away, swallowing the air in huge gulps, I finally reached the summit, unsteadily turned around on wobbly legs, and released my mind completely on the effortless way to the bottom. My brain was mush. I floated my last lap downhill, relishing the warm relaxing sensation which set in as I rested exhaustedly on a guard rail by the roadside. Sweat poured from my skin, but all I could feel was the warmth as my euphoric soul drifted high above the city. The torture was over for now.

The road I run on sits right on the hillside, such that I have a wonderful view of the setting sun and the oncoming clouds in the west, and the sparkling city view to the southeast. The air was a crisp, fresh contrast to my sweaty, overheated body and the clean breeze reminded me of the autumn nights we had in New England as the maples leaves were turning. The clarity of the view—the sky awash with streams of brilliant yellow, orange, and purple; the thin layer of pure white clouds overlying the distant, blue Pacific—was courtesy of one of those rare but magical surprise showers we do get on occasion in southern California.

I sat quietly, breathing deeply, content and tranquil with my endorphic high, staring through the wisps of passing clouds into the darkening skies toward the fast-fading, late afternoon sun. The sky seemed to sink right into the ocean and the hint of horizon continued endlessly as far as I could see. I breathed in again. Light travels forever, I thought. I could hear my heart pound rapidly, reliably. What I see is infinity.

As boy scout campers, we used to shine flashlights into the heavens above and wonder how far the light could travel after we turned it off. Of course the light, as defined by light waves, traveled forever although its ever-expanding beam would soon dissipate into infinite space and be lost to the human eye. It boggled my mind to think that light could theoretically, if not practically, travel forever and expand to infinity. And it was equally incomprehensible thinking in terms of the millions or billions or trillions of light-years which were already expanding toward infinity.

This evening was no exception. Not only did the idea of light traveling forever come to mind, but because of the heavenly spectacle, the question of why clouds exist, or rather, how clouds exist and how they die entered my mind. I'm not talking in the meteorological sense but in a perceptive way.

I watched the various types and formations of clouds move through the multi-colored sky. There were the fine wisps, which seemed motionless as if lightly brushed onto the blue canvas by an artist's hand. The light subtly reflected off these cotton strands as it does a woman's hair as she lies asleep during an afternoon nap.

Then there were the dense, compact wads of clouds that blew past me overhead. These light gray, agitated masses, opaque in the middle but less well defined around the edges, hovered ominously over my dampened head like wrathful mistresses before moving on in a burst of wind.

Finally, in the distance, settling over the Santa Monica Bay and the Marina Harbor, were massive, majestic plumes of maternal cumulus clouds, dazzling white with the reflected setting sunlight. These huge cotton balls appeared immobile, as if standing guard over the waters and the delicate wisps below.

As I took in this stunning scene, I wondered what caused one cloud to be so different from another just a few hundred feet away. It is too easy to say there are inversion layers here and temperature differences there. I was speaking about change on a microscopic level. Why does this molecule of water congregate near another and what would cause it to move away, and thus change the shape or size of the cloud? What makes the molecules change in such a way that they eventually, and inevitably, disappear? And why? Even clouds don't live forever.

It is obvious that the Chinese live in China and Indians live in India, but how did Mr. and Mrs. Chang come to live next to Mr. and Mrs. Gandhi in West Los Angeles? How did a fat, brainy Chinese kid from Quincy turn into a slightly less fat, slightly less brainy Chinese man-child in Beverly Hills? You get my drift. The constant, ever-changing micromovement is just as bewildering as the more obvious macromovement. What moves things to move and, thus, change?

"Forever," "infinity," and "infinitely small" are mind-blowing concepts to me. Forever-and-ever would seem to be doubly confusing, if that is possible. It is like contemplating a never-ending Mobius strip or counting grains of sand or the stars above. Each little bit of infinity is made up of something infinitely small. Together they make up forever. At some point, the brain has to turn off or we would go crazy with the impossibility of the concept. But sometimes, it pays to think about it.

I used to try to think of the number of chickens killed each day to feed the world's population and what that would mean in terms of the number and mass of chickens that have passed through this world since the beginning of time. I could never get a handle on that finite number, but I imagine it would be quite a bit more than even the number of Big Macs sold which, in and of itself, is a hell of a big number. Most people care only about the chicken on their own plates.

I'm not sure why I started contemplating this. Perhaps it was that a triweekly jog is so finite. It starts with the mind and body in one state and ends with the mind and body in another. The beginning is a simple step forward and the end is when the body collapses to a standstill. Yet in between is a whole different life. And light from the sun seems to have no finite beginning or end and clouds seem to be in a constant state of inexplicable metamorphosis. They don't die. They just fade away until we can't call them clouds anymore.

Perhaps the reason I contemplated all this was that my brain was lacking oxygen.

My life on earth—in fact, *all* life, at one time—seemed to be like my jog. It began at some definable point long before I was ever aware of "being." And I always assumed that it would end just as definitively as when I sat my exhausted butt heavily against the cold metallic guard rail. Life and death seemed pretty clear at one point in life.

Through the years, I had to learn that this was really not the case. The issue of the definition of the beginning of human life is one that is being challenged in all arenas of our society, even to the absurd end of arguing whether sperm have rights.

Similarly, the finality of death is suspect. It's amazing that theologians, ethicists, neurologists, psychologists, ECG and EEG technicians, attorneys, judges, and senators all may have a say in who is dead and who is not. And the science of cryogenics makes things even more hazy.

Despite its pain and simplicity, there is something quite elegant and reassuring about a jog with its limitation on time and space. Even if I could, I wouldn't want to jog forever. And at the same time, I am enamored with, and in awe of, the foreverness of the sun's rays or the infinite variations of a cloud's form. I find that beautiful and hypnotic. That is where life is really lived and appreciated—at the fringes, at the head of the ray or the edge of a cloud.

Way back in grade school, I learned about the googol—a one with a hundred zeros after it. Just like the glittering lights of the city below, while it seems unfathomably large, it is finite. If I had an infinite amount of time, I could start with one and end with a googol. Now that doesn't attract me as a reason to live any more than does taking an accurate census of all the light bulbs in Los Angeles. But it is comforting to know that I could potentially manage a concept which at first presents itself as an impossible task. The battle of the conceivable versus the inconceivable stimulates the basic intrigue of human nature and instinct. That is what magic, entertainment, wonderment, and dreams are made of. It is what makes humans unique among God's creatures.

I drew in a deep breath to calm my pounding heart. Between inspiration and expiration is an ill-defined state where I am not holding my breath or breathing or dead. It occurs twice with each cycle of breathing. I need each part of the cycle for life to continue, but at the end of each part, I am flirting with the part we call death or suspended animation. Life is filled with inspiration and ends with expiration. Too much of either can kill you.

Death was really *not* what I was feeling after this jog, although it might have seemed like an inevitable event during the trudge to the top. Instead, it was *life* that I was sucking in with each labored inspiration. I was inhaling the edge of the cloud and burning with the head of the ray. I couldn't run forever, but I did think about living forever even while knowing I never could and never would. Some part of me wanted to find out how to run and jog forever and ever, another wanted to just lie down and stare at the clouds overhead.

As I thought about all of these silly concepts, glad to be alone with these secrets, I remembered a paradox with which every child is probably familiar. This paradox has a tendency to humble my wits and irritate my nerves.

The paradox goes something like this: If you are standing in front of a wall, you know it is a simple matter to walk over and reach the wall. Yet in order to reach the wall, you must travel at least half the distance. Once you have attained that halfway point, there will be another halfway point. As soon as you have reached the second halfway point, there will be another. And on and on and on. Ad infinitum. For every distance, no matter how small there will be a halfway point to reach. The wall, however close we get, can never, theoretically, be reached.*

---

*This is the famous Zeno's paradox

So we are caught in a trap of never being able to reach the wall. There is an infinite number of halfway points. And if we push the paradox the other way, we would never be able to move at all since in order to get to the first halfway point there would be another halfway point before it, and another halfway point before that halfway point. And on and on and on. Ad infinitum. Simply put, we are immobile—and as good as dead.

Of course, the solution to the original paradox is that even though the process of halving the distance can go on forever, the actual distance becomes infinitely small and the time it takes to cross that distance becomes infinitely short. Mathematically speaking, infinity x 1/infinity equals one. The other solution is simply to walk over to the wall and kick a hole in it for causing such grief in the first place.

I picked myself up from the guard rail and walked exhaustedly to my front door. The cold air had tightened my leg muscles a bit and my back had begun to stiffen. My walk was unsteady and hesitant. I just wanted to rest for a long time. As the image of the paradox flashed through my mind, I wondered if the inability to move an infinitesimal distance could paralyze me forever. I worried that the paradox might one day become truth. I took one final inspiration from the autumn air, looked at the ever-changing clouds swirling about my head, and passed definitively through the door. So much for that paradox!

The aggravating thing about paradoxes is that they sound so logical. They won't go away. You can dissect them over and over again and they won't die. They are truly forever. They challenge reality and force you to reexamine what is truth.

Somewhere beneath my cold and clammy skin was a nagging hope that perhaps there was yet another halfway point in my half-over life. And another beyond that. And on and on and on. And one form of my living will be transformed into another form. And another beyond that. And on and on and on. Ad infinitum. Because I love the sun's rays and I love the cloud's edge. And I hate to jog—unless it's on the road at the very top of the world.

12

Life Is But a Dream

I was lamenting the other day that I don't dream anymore. At least I hardly ever remember my dreams. I have always envied people who had vivid dreams they could clearly relate the following morning as much as I admire friends who can tell a good joke the day after they've heard it. A good joke told over again enhances the quality of life and, in dreaming, people are able to extend their conscious life by living during the time they sleep. And what healthy, sane person doesn't want to increase his or her lifespan?

I'm certainly not an expert on dreams, but I do know they play important roles in our lives. Dreams may serve a variety of purposes from release of tension and stress, to liberation of our subconscious mind, to exercising our imagination and reinforcing our memories. Many dreams are revealing. Some are frightening. Most are just plain nonsense.

The single most frightening thing about my earlier dreams was the sense of fear and anxiety I felt when I was physically immobilized. Everyone knows what that is like: the "get out of the way the train is about to hit me but I can't move" feeling. The mind is willing but the flesh is paralyzed. It is as if the conscious brain is dissociated from the unconscious body. All volition and control of one's life is lost. It may not even involve an impending or even a clearly defined danger, only the threat of not being able to get out of the nightmare, an inability to escape. The dissociated out-of-body experience, that is, the sense of paralysis, is itself a dissociated out-of-body experience viewed from a subconscious distance. Awareness is depersonalized: "That can't be me lying on the tracks!" But I know it is, even if it really isn't. The feelings are all too real, so real that sometimes I have awakened to sounds of myself sobbing with fear and frustration.

Just as frustrating is the inability to climb back into a great dream which is so rich that it becomes real. It's like great entertainment. Sometimes, the adventure and sexual potential is so great, reality itself becomes the enemy. We don't want to wake up. Sometimes great things happen. You get to visit other worlds and interact with people and things you never imagined while awake. You become a totally different person. These dreams are cliffhangers that we don't want to end but which inevitably get cancelled in mid-show. The wind rattles the door or the phone rings. No matter how hard I try to get back into the dream, to relive the fantasy, once I am roused, the episode is gone forever. All I am left with is a head full of frustration and sheets wet with sweat.

I'd love to describe my most vivid episodes, if only I could remember them. Actions, I forget. Feelings, I remember. It's odd how fantasy in an unconscious state can make life such a dream.

Like many people's, my dreams were often extensions of my waking present. Frequently, they were more compelling than everyday life. They were free movies (always with a seat reserved especially for me), a kind of unconscious virtual reality. A reality that I tried to control; in some ways, the best kind of reality.

I have a feeling that humans can live with only so much fantasy. Those with dull, monotonous lives will have a tendency to seek out fantasy in real life or through dreams. Those with rich, active lives will use sleep periods to rest their overheated minds. People can't live a life of total fantasy, or else they'll go crazy.

This theory of balanced fantasy is evident in schizophrenia. An average person who is sleep-deprived, when allowed to return to sleep, will enter early and prolonged rapid eye movement sleep (REM rebound) where dreams occur. Active schizophrenics do not experience REM rebound. The conclusion is that schizophrenics live out their fantasy in real life via psychotic hallucinations and thus do not need the fantasy of dreams. Treated schizophrenics experience REM rebound like normal people. Suppressing the fantasy in conscious life forces fantasy to occur in sleep.

I don't consider myself particularly schizophrenic but I do not seem to dream as vigorously or as often as the average person, and certainly not as much as I'd like to. Even as a teenager, and even more so as a college student, lacking spontaneous dreams, I would go to my bed at night trying to "force" a dream of my own design. Sometimes I could actually generate a dream very close to what I wanted to "see." These dreams blended into what any sane person would refer to as "wishful thinking." Freud made a whole career out of these dreams. And I wanted those dreams. I needed them.

Friends and relatives have said that my head was always full of ideas and thought, wondering and imagining things. What went on during the day just blended into what I wanted to go on in the night when my mind was supposed to be at rest. As opposed to the simply busy body who needs to put his brain to sleep at night, my dreamingly busy body sought to continue dreaming at night. I suspect everyone does this to a certain degree, like dreaming about the girl or boy you just met in English class but were afraid to ask out on a date. When life itself is so interesting, you don't want to go to sleep. Ask any eight-year-old.

Many of these subconscious dramas had to do with celebrating heroism, charisma, and popularity, many of the characteristics I thought I lacked and privately craved. I was usually a savior of sorts, rescuing a damsel in distress. I was forever getting these poor women into the worst binds with every type of evil scoundrel and malicious force I could conjure up: sometimes dragons, other times bullies, but generally anyone who wasn't me. Then I'd play the hero and rescue them. Often these damsels were no one in particular—simply generically beautiful women—although specific women I coveted in real life would sneak into these dreams quite easily.

Most of the time, I forced certain dreams because I was feeling sorry for myself about something or secretly thought of something I wasn't able to express in real life. It was less the woman and more my ego that was the lead character. As often as not, dreams did not include women, but, rather, situations such as hitting home runs or being elected President of the United States or sinking free throws to win world championships.

I admit that some of the "dreams" were geeky by today's standards. Chess games and violin concerts were frequent arenas. Here, I played before thousands of adoring fans. Women were particularly impressed by my feats. That was as certain as my waking up in the morning.

I never felt embarrassed or self-conscious about these dreams because no one ever knew. That is the terrific thing about dreams. They are completely inviolable and private. They are events to look forward to and try to cultivate. Being less heroic or masculine in real life, like most people, I relied on my forced dreams to take on a realism of their own. The surprising thing about all of this is that the dreams generally made me feel more heroic and masculine without actually having to be so. I just knew that I was because my dreams were proof. I didn't feel the need to be that way in real life. It was the "if he said that to me I'd bop him one but he didn't so I don't have to" mentality. It gave me a sense of self-confidence that is too hard to earn outside of these dreams. Everyone should try it.

Dreams, when they occurred, were good to me back then. I don't remember any bad dreams except the ones in which I was immobilized. Looking back on the dreams I had as an adolescent, many of the wishful-thinking dreams germinated from a subconscious sense of inferiority, or at least a fear of inferiority, and a depression of sorts because of that fear. The dreams served a tremendously beneficial purpose in allowing me to adjust to and work out my real-life fears and frustrations within the context of my private fantasies. I always won the game and got the girl, unless the train was on the way.

Where life ends and dreams begin cannot always be answered clearly. During my surgical residency, a time when I had quite a few dreams because of sleep-deprivation, I once bolted from my deep slumber, threw on some scrubs, and raced three miles down Pacific Coast Highway in my car, getting halfway to UCLA Medical Center before I had this odd suspicion that the emergency phone call I thought I had received from some excitable nurse was merely a dream. I argued with myself for another three miles along Sunset Boulevard about the possibility of this dream *not* being a dream since it felt so convincingly real. The thought of bursting into the intensive care unit in a frenzy, ready to tackle a life-threatening situation and having the nurses stare at me like the idiotic ignoramus most greenhorn residents like me were, led me to confirm with the hospital page operator that I was indeed dreaming. That one phone call saved me months of embarrassment. But I still could've sworn it was real.

Another time, I was attending a poolside cocktail party on the island of Kauai. Very chic! It was during my college years and I had just traveled cross-country with a friend by car and had flown to Hawaii. Having had little sleep and being totally exhausted, I tried to make small talk with strangers. I was standing six feet from the end of a huge pool in this beautiful tropical setting, a well-heeled crowd buzzing about in colorful, floral evening wear, the warm ocean air and light dancing off the water hypnotizing me.

Holding a glass of gin and tonic as a prop, I hadn't taken more than a few sips. Half a drink into the conversation, I began to feel extremely drowsy and found myself leaning ever so slightly away from my conversation partner. Much like sinking into a restful slumber, I did a graceful, reverse swan dive into the pool and quickly sank to the bottom.

From then on, I had a feeling of being in a peaceful dream, perhaps like the sensation a person might have when he or she decides to give up the ghost. Every muscle of my body was totally relaxed. I felt content. I remember the sensation of floating, half thinking I was drowning and half believing I was still alive. Somehow it didn't even feel like me. Neither the exhaustion nor the highly chlorinated water seemed to matter. I knew there was a danger, but at the same time, felt that nothing could really hurt me. I actually saw the famous bright light at the end of the proverbial tunnel, although it might have been the lanterns hanging over the pool as my face stared at the water's undersurface. It seemed to be getting closer and closer. It seemed to take forever. Even though I was an underwater swimming champion at summer camp as a boy, swimming at least two and a half full lengths of the pool in one breath, I didn't believe I could actually hold my breath for such a long time. I remember my lungs weren't burning as they should. It was almost as if I didn't even need oxygen. I continued drifting toward the light in slow motion. It was a peaceful ride devoid of all sound.

Being dissociated from the act of drowning, I was just in another dream where I was incapable of effecting the necessary action to avoid disaster. My muscles were limp. My mind told me I shouldn't be in this situation. I remembered that I had been standing next to the pool and now I was in over my head with all this water. This didn't make sense. I wanted to escape the dream. I had to get out of the pool. The oncoming train . . .

Thanks to a couple of brave bus boys who decided such a stupid joke could go on only so long before it was no longer a joke, I am still here to relate this "dream." I suppose the people who didn't know it wasn't a prank thought it was pretty funny. I thought it was one of the most remarkable dreams I ever had.

It is easy to blame these dreams on stress, sleep-deprivation, and run-of-the-mill exhaustion, but it is not so easy to relate each and every dream or nightmare to a relevant aspect of one's life at a particular time. Nor would one necessarily want to. I am not so preoccupied with what I dream. Nor should anyone be. But dreams, or the act of dreaming as a whole, must have meaning for each of us. The act of dreaming takes up 50 percent of an infant's life, but less and less of an aging adult's. The fact that I am having fewer of these meaningful encounters must itself mean something. And that is what bothers me now.

This may not be an earth-shattering revelation to anyone since this is what shrinks do every day. But as I have never been to a shrink, this self-realization is a wonder to me. Most people halfway through life have spent almost half of that life unconscious in sleep and in dreams. How that private life of dreams is lived should be almost as important as the conscious life. After all, how do we know that what we accept as real is really real?

That brings me to my dreamless state. Somewhere between wishful thinking and half dead, dreams are being lost. Why don't I dream anymore? Could it have to do more with my memory than dreaming itself? What can I do to bring those dreams, even those nightmares, back?

Cynics (of whom I often am one) may say, why worry about dreams when one should be worried about life? Pessimists (of whom there are many) may wonder, why lament nightmares you need not face? Realists (to whom none of this means much) may argue that dreams don't amount to anything but illusions. But artists (whom we all have the potential to be) thrive on dreams.

I suppose that is what all of this is about: the firm belief in the art of living and the artistry of life. What is real is not. And what appears not to be is. Life is much more than what the living live. The Belgian artist René Magritte illustrated as much with his painting of a pipe and the inscription underneath contradicting the obvious: "This is not a pipe." Life is but a dream, and dreams are life. Anything we can squeeze out of life, whatever we can dream, we should. Why be content with only half a life?

Dreams, which I only now understand as having a constructive place in my life, are important. I'm sure that a few thousand dollars of therapy would have led me to the same conclusion much more quickly, but perhaps with less satisfaction than of having discovered it myself.

I do miss dreaming. Lately, though, since starting this chapter, the dreams have become more frequent and certainly more vivid. This is God's way of keeping me honest. Just when I think I've found a solution and understand the problem, life changes and I realize I didn't have a problem at all. Magritte himself never felt compelled to explain everything about reality, but only to question it.

There is no question that I am happier knowing that dreams do still come to me. For a while I was worried. I'll be even more happy if I can conjure up dreams as I did before; to feel the sweat of the game and the breath of a sweet maiden; to smile at the beautiful strains of my violin in some great concert hall and, yes, even feel the chilling fear of immobility; to wish one night, I might be able to leap back into the dream, into the illusory river of emotions and events; to be a hero and savior and pray that I can escape the grasp of that impending doom. For dreams are not only a relief from living, they are life itself and glimpses into what is possible.

13

Memory

We all are blessed with memory, some more than others. Most memory is subconscious. Some is intentional. Unfortunately, it's is one of those things we notice most when we can't seem to find it.

As a child, I had a photographic memory. One of my favorite pastimes in junior high school was playing chess during free periods. I was a decent player—not great, but competitive. Although I didn't study chess like some whizzes and didn't spend the time to analyze the game and its conventions, I did have a knack for intuitively thinking many steps ahead of each move, which is essential to being a good player. I loved luring my opponent into believing I was trapped or so stupid as to give up a rook for a knight and enjoyed smiling when they irreversibly fell into the trap I had set for them.

Much of the ability to form strategies and to play a multi-dimensional game had to do with concentration. Throughout my life, I only knew how to perform with a singular mental commitment. Every action that had a perceptible intellectualized root was purposeful. My father's "What's the purpose?" echoed often if not quietly. I did not sacrifice a rook without a reason, even if that reason was that I had not seen a trap set for me by my opponent.

Because our free periods in junior high school were only about forty-five minutes long, most chess games that were started in one period had to be continued into the following day or week. We couldn't save the board. They had to be wiped clean for the next group of students. At the end of each free period, before putting the men away into their wooden boxes, I would have to remember where every piece was so I could set the same game a few days later. Since I concentrated so hard, not so much to remember the position of each piece solely as a mnemonic exercise, but to increase my chances of trapping my opponent in some devious strategic plot, reconstructing the game board was not that difficult. The amazing thing to me now (and I say this with self-effacement) is that I memorized not one, but two, boards at once since I usually played simultaneously with two different opponents.

I'm sure some people will think, "How arrogant!" But I didn't do this to show off. I just wanted to play with more than one friend at a time during what always seemed to be too short a free period. At any rate, my photographic memory came in very handy and enhanced my intellectual reputation, as well as my own self-confidence, during this crucial period of my life. I'm certain people think that if you can play two simultaneous games of chess, remember the position of every piece for a few days, and win most of the time, you must be pretty damn smart. Besides, few, if any, of the other students had the ability to question my memory in any serious way when it came to chess.

To be sure, many kids had the same or even superior ability to remember things other than positions of chessmen: Mickey Mantle's batting statistics, the dialogue to a hit movie, our parents' promises bartered for a task well done. "But you *said* you'd pay a dollar for every A!"

Music is the universal memory enhancer. Melodies and lyrics seem to stick much more easily than the elemental chemistry chart, which is why someone cleverly composed a song reciting the entire elemental chart. Too bad I can't remember it.

As a violinist who learned how to read music early on, the photographic memory allowed me to play music literally (i.e., by memory), by picturing the sheet of music in my head and "playing" directly from that visualization. I actually "saw" the page. To do this takes a different neurological pathway than to simply play from memory. The former follows a visual pathway while the other follows a presumably auditory or tactile pathway of memory.

The need to memorize music, as well as to remember how to play the actual instrument in the necessary manner to produce the music, stimulated the memorization function of my brain. In general, when playing music, memory was second nature. Memorizing a Mozart concerto was a given. Playing it so that it sounded how Mozart intended it to sound was the real challenge. Even now, I take for granted that a youngster can effortlessly play a long and complicated piece of music from memory. I assume the child's mind is like a sponge that laps up anything the external world throws at it. To see some children play music, you'd think they were recording machines.

■   ■   ■

My memory started to deteriorate about the time I was aware of my memorization skills and of the cerebral functions of which I was capable. I don't mean this to say that I was such an extraordinary genius or savant. In fact, I was never really convinced of my intellect as much as my peers and elders were. But when I became very conscious, in the clinical sense, of what I was doing and how and why, the abilities to do so seemed to evaporate. Innate ability may be hampered by too much awareness.

In particular, my photographic memory started to fail me somewhere in my late teens—fairly early, I thought, for senility to set in. Memorizing music became almost impossible, no matter how hard I tried. Pieces that I played so effortlessly, even if a little tonally inaccurate, would not stay put in my mind. The fingerings on my violin, which previously flowed smoothly even while daydreaming, needed to be consciously committed to memory. This detracted from the very ability to commit them to memory. In short, I had to try too hard to memorize. I no longer had the confidence to perform in public from memory because I knew I had the ability to forget. The more you know, the more you can forget, and the less you know that you know.

I suppose this is a species of stage fright, but in a very global and generic sense as far as memory is concerned. Lyrics to songs wouldn't stick. Names of people I just met went in one ear and out the other. Poetry had to be less than two lines long. My secret dream of becoming an actor like John Wayne or Errol Flynn remained a closeted fantasy for fear of forgetting my lines.

Although I did okay during the intervening years in a field in which

memory had always carried a premium value, I was very aware of this decline in aptitude. I'm sure that there were thousands of things that I continued to commit to memory quite easily. These were undoubtedly things
that had intrinsic value to me, such as a favorite girlfriend's phone number, the myriad of risks and caveats in an informed consent of a prospec-
tive patient, or the exact price at which I bought each stock in my meager portfolio. But now, memorization does not come as effortlessly and
subconsciously as when I was a child. Thinking and memorization were
almost synonymous then. Every time my brain turned on and something
was inputted, it stuck. I remembered the starting lineup of the 1960
Boston Red Sox even though I didn't have to. Now I have to flog my brain
to remember what to order once I've put the menu down. And this only
worsens with time.

Why this was happening always nagged me. I knew my intellect per
se had not declined significantly. I could certainly grasp complicated
concepts like anaerobic metabolism and multidimensional reconstructive
surgery. I knew my world had not become less interesting to me, but
more. And I knew that in my constant search for the truth and the commonality of life, things and events were all relevant in some way to my
life and outlook on life. No, there had to be an organic reason for this feeling of memory loss. Everybody is looking for it because everybody needs
something to blame it on.

While I am acutely aware of the fact that my memory is not as keen
as when I was a growing child, it never really bothered me until recently.
Previously, as soon as I had realized I had forgotten something or was unable to remember another thing, I was off on a different thought. I quickly
forgot that I had forgotten. As we grow up and mature, our life and environment usually broaden. Our life gets cluttered with "stuff," as one famous comedian calls it. Important "stuff," mundane "stuff," unusual
"stuff," petty "stuff." Just a lot of "stuff." All this "stuff"and how we deal
with this "stuff" is what we call life. Memorization becomes less of a task
than a tool to deal with "stuff."

We are no longer called upon to recite the twelve cranial nerves,
twelve disciples, or seven dwarfs. Most of us no longer need to perform
Mozart from memory or recite a Shakespearean sonnet. Instead, memory
is used subconsciously in a system of rational thought to achieve a goal
beyond that of memory itself. In surgery, one does not memorize the

steps to an operation like the gifts of the twelve (or is it ten?) days of Christmas. We become aware of the various steps because they rationally fit together to accomplish the task efficiently. One doesn't cook by memory. One cooks when memory becomes secondary.

Of course this explanation doesn't satisfy me at all since it is more of an explanation or excuse than a solution. I still can't remember the second verse to "Mary Had a Little Lamb" or "Rock-a-Bye-Baby." Parents with little babies know all the verses. But that's a lot to ask just to improve memory.

Some say you know you are getting old if all you have are memories. So, unsentimental people vow never to live life for the memories, never to have their lives filled only by memories, never to look back. But the fact of the matter is that we *do* look back and, in fact, we *should*. Our lives are constantly being filled with memories, both intended and unintended, and there will be times when we would like to remember "the time when. . . ." Memory is one of the great learning tools and joys of life itself. When it is gone, we might as well pack it in.

That is the underlying fear of memory loss. Just ask someone with a true memory loss or dramatic decline in memory capacity. The only thing worse to me is having a memory but not the able body. That is like being a neurologist. You can know exactly what is happening and why, and even what should be done to cure it; but you can't do anything about it because you don't have the tools.

■　　■　　■

A long time back, I suppose when I first became aware of my loss of potential for memorization, perhaps during medical school when memorization was pushed to its limits, I looked a bit into what memory is exactly. Why is there long-term and short-term memory? Why is a child more easily able to memorize than an adult? Why can I remember a hundred phone numbers but not my driver's license number? Why am I so upset that I can't remember the names of the girls I've dated or the one-line joke I heard in a play a week ago?

My brain can't be much more different than that of the next guy. We both have trillions of brain cells. Certainly that is enough. And whether memory is a molecule, a chemical change, or a neural pathway, unless there is a disease or anomaly occurring in my head, we should have similar capacities for memory. But lately, it seems as if I am forever trying, however futilely, to dredge up memories from a distant past or chastising myself for not remembering an event my father remembered from last year or a scene from a movie a friend swears we saw last month.

It won't surprise me that those same people, if they are preoccupied enough to think about it, are saying the same things to themselves. "What happened to my memory?"

Therein lies the key: few people are preoccupied with memory. In some respects, it matters little to me what the physiological basis of memory is, whether it is a molecule or a pathway. I'm not about to stock up on vitamin E or tryptophan or stand on my head to increase blood flow to the cerebral cortex. It matters even less to me that the next person is or is not concerned about losing memory or even whether or not he truly is. But I do care about myself and what memory means to me. Everyone should. Memory is intimately tied to emotion. We memorize as children because the ability to so do is rewarded or deterred and that reward or deterrent is related to an emotional sense of well-being and pride, pain and hurt. We regret the inability to remember as adults, because we crave the emotions the memories bring and the mere satisfaction that one can indeed still remember.

What each individual thinks about memory is a piece of that very same person. That he doesn't want a bag of memories at life's end says something. That he fears those memories indicates something. That he doesn't care about looking back at his childhood to learn about his adulthood means something. That he can't remember his in-laws and their birthdays says a lot—and it ain't good!

Outside of memorizing for memories' sake, I always believed that memorization occurred naturally when there was a reason to commit something to memory. That is, one memorizes either because it is intrinsically easy to do, because one concentrates hard enough, or because it is consciously or subconsciously meaningful. Important things were easy to memorize. Unimportant things were not. So it is twice as frustrating when we tell ourselves, "This is a moment to savor. This is something worth remembering." And then we forget. . . .

■ ■ ■

During residency, every resident carried cards to record important details on each patient—details such as history, pertinent exam findings, key lab values, and test results. These cards were the lifelines of the patients who were dependent on these young residents to care for them. The cards were also insurance for residents against embarrassment, ignorance, and screwups. Every resident had a stack of these cards in his or her white coat pocket ready at hand. Having chief residents or attending surgeons berate you in front of patients and nurses for not having crucial or, for that matter, even trivial data was one of the least memorable experiences in medical training. No one went through residency without these cards. No one, that is, but me.

I figured that if it wasn't important, it wasn't worth writing down. And if it was important, I'd remember it. By not having the cards to refer to, just like not looking at sheet music when playing Mozart, I tuned into the patients as human beings more quickly and was able to "play" the patient with more sensitivity and understanding. My capacity for memory and the need to memorize seemed fairly evenly matched because it was meaningful. Besides, it was more of a challenge to put all that stuff in my brain and not in my coat pocket.

It appears as if, through the years, my memory cup leaketh out. I retain less and less of what I want to. Things I used to remember have spilled out onto the floor of life. Things I want to remember trickle away to evaporate into my past.

But each frame of life is worthy of memory because each second of life has the potential to be worth two seconds of life. One second for life itself, and another second for the memories when life winds down.

One can make love for the moment or one can make love for the moment *and* savor it as memory the next day. Any loss of memory potential is loss of life itself. Sometimes this is good, like a beating victim who can't remember the horrors of the beating or a child who has permanent amnesia for the events of abuse. But most of the time, in most lives that are filled with beautiful and wonderful things, loss of memory is a waste.

So what are we to do with the apparent loss of memory besides admire the likes of Zino Francescatti, who had memorized fifty major violin concertos, any one of which he could play with brilliance at a drop of the baton from a conductor? One thing is to realize that it is truly only an apparent loss of memory in most cases, including my own. I have not really lost any memory potential. It's only that I was fooled long ago into believing that I had any extraordinary potential to begin with. At certain stages in life, one has very little to memorize. I only needed to remember the positions of my rooks and knights. I didn't care about the stock market, Chinese politics, fifty nurses, doctors and patients, what I am going to say at an upcoming lecture or what to do when the Big One strikes.

I have also not lost any memory. I just don't remember where I left it. Eventually, when the moment requires it, like the lab values on the nonexistent cheat card, I'll remember. I'll mop up the memories and squeeze them back into the cup of life.

The other thing is to accept that everything we do in the many frames of life, we do because of its relative importance. Going to the grocery store, for the most part, is not important until it becomes necessary. These events are forgettable, which is why most guys forget exactly what the girls tell us to get. But most encounters with people, whether they be patients, nurses, doctors, friends, relatives, the guy on the street, or a girl behind the counter—most of these encounters are important because that is life that cannot be bought or manufactured. They deserve to be remembered in some way: perhaps the smell, the idea, the look, the feeling. All these things go into my memory bank to be lost among the positions of all the pawns and devious strategies.

In the end, no matter who you are, there is a limit to what you can remember. When you want to remember everything, you're bound to forget something. When you have basically nothing to remember, you probably won't forget much.

It's a little like baseball. The guys who pitched the most games lost the most and the guys who batted the most struck out the most. But all these players ended up in the Hall of Fame because they were also the winningest and most productive players in the game.

So, rather then spend the rest of my memory potential lamenting the loss of memory, I am content to know that I miss my memory because I want to remember so much and, indeed, have so much to remember. I want to stuff my memory bank with all there is in life. I want my cup to runneth over and over and over. The alternative to this strategy is too painful to consider, especially when I remember how good it was to win all those chess games a long time ago.

14

Devouring Oneself

Like most people, I am a relatively upstanding citizen. I am loath to litter. I freeze curbside when "Don't Walk" flashes. I pay my taxes and I always correct a waiter's mistake even when it costs me money. But I have one uncontrollable, despicable, destructive habit, one that I've had since early on, one that I'm often ashamed to admit. I bite my fingernails.

I can't remember ever sucking my thumb and I'm not flexible enough to reach my toes. But chewing on my fingernails is as familiar to me as overeating. It is so natural to jam my fingernails against my central incisors and nip off the offensive tips of each nail until the plate lies flush to the flesh. Most of the time I spit out the specimen like an annoying seed in a seedless fruit, but occasionally I have the irresistible urge to morselize the crescent-shaped clipping and swallow it whole. Loose bits of dead skin hanging from the cuticles are also ready tidbits. It is part grooming, part entertainment, part habit. Even in grade school my fingernails were jagged and embarrassing. It didn't occur to me until much later that not only was this habit fairly disgusting, but also, in a way, undeniably self-destructive.

My mother used to chastise me severely. "Dei Dei, quit biting your nails!" she'd harangue. But what were mothers for? I didn't take the admonition that seriously. Joanne, my wife, takes great personal pride in yelling at me because she is so nauseated by the thought and sight of my filthy fingernails in my filthy mouth. "Robin, that's so disgusting! Didn't your mother ever teach you anything? Do you know how many germs there are under your nails? Do you know how dirty money is? Weren't you just picking your toes? How can you put your fingers in your mouth?" Unfortunately, she is so fastidious and pathologically hygienic that it is itself nauseating to listen to her tirades. It soon goes in one ear and out the other. Besides, there are less virile germs on my hand than in my mouth.

I suppose the original habit was a product of nervousness or boredom. Maybe ignorance made me do it. Now perhaps it's just the pressures of decisions. Occasionally it's rebellion or pure hedonism. Sometimes it just feels sooo . . . good.

Fortunately neither my mother nor my wife has ever seen patients who are afflicted with a pathological craving to eat their own flesh, usually biting their lips and mouth until they bleed. The Lesch-Nyhan Syndrome is a genetic trait that produces a compulsion in the young to devour themselves without regard to self-preservation. These children end up with large deformities of the mouth and fingers because of this autocannibalism. They literally eat away at themselves. They may bleed and contract infections and inflict on themselves chronic, nonhealing wounds, but the deformities are limited to the face and hands so they don't die of this bizarre behavior. At least *they* have a genetic excuse. What's so disturbing is that these patients know what they are doing, but can't stop themselves. It's a compulsion, involuntary. It's not because they are stupid.

■   ■   ■

So comes this mid-life tale that you can choose to ignore as fable or take to heart as fact concerning someone who has the same habit I have of biting and swallowing fingernails. I have seen this incessant nibbling of cuticles, calluses, fingertips, and keratin. All these various pieces of human anatomy are delicately masticated and swallowed like hors d'oeuvres at a cocktail party. It seems so matter-of-fact and inconsequential, since all of these things are quite dead, usually without virtue, and no one is hurt by this peculiarity. It never occurred to me that this was anything more than a nauseating annoyance. I never thought it could eventually destroy the world.

Then one day it seemed something was terribly amiss. A bandage, crimson with fresh, sticky blood, was wrapped tightly around a pinky. It appeared as if the habit did not stop at the tips of the fingernails. Today, it had run amuck and progressed down the little finger of the left hand to the second knuckle.

I admit I was startled. Not so much because of the blood, for it was not that much, nor the fact that the habit had gotten a little out of hand (pardon the pun), but mainly because no one else said anything about it. The bandaged hand was taken with casual acceptance and life continued. Social etiquette probably dictated that one keep his or her mouth shut when one isn't involved with such attention-getting behavior. As a young child, though, I would have at least stared with my mouth open.

Soon the wound healed and nothing was ever said. A missing finger is not that unusual for an adult and it was the nondominant hand, so that the incapacitation was very slight if any. But soon after, the other pinky and forefinger received bandages—presumably for the same reason. Still no one dared inquire. Eyes turned away. Life went on.

Madness comes in many forms and I assumed that this was just one manifestation. We all get carried away with things we take for granted. Obsessions creep up and overtake us before we are even aware of the habit. A two-dollar bet on a Derby horse can lead to destitution, and a love of art or a woman can leave one putting an ear in an envelope. As a doctor, I've been exposed to enough in the first half of life to take many extraordinary events stoically. I've seen grown men go mad with anger or pain in emergency rooms, destroying anything within reach. I've had patients, riddled with a dozen senseless bullets, die with my hands in their lifeless cavities. I've had a patient overrun with hepatitis, TB, syphilis, *and* AIDS macheted nearly in two for want of a five-dollar bill. So, like everyone around me, I went on with my own business and tried to ignore this latest social aberration. I did, however, make a mental note to myself to protest loudly if *my* pinky ever ended up at the tips of someone else's incisors.

Weeks passed and the fingertips healed as always. Since human beings are not salamanders, reminders of this behavior greeted me daily although all other outward signs suggested nothing but a friendly and benign disposition. Springtime lifted spirits beyond any possible sinister thought. The days warmed and greenery began to return. The birds began to sing and the butterflies lighted on the wild poppies. And life went on.

Then thinness began to set in. Nothing dramatic or extraordinary—just an insidious, barely perceptible, but measurable thinness: the eye sockets became more hollow, the temples narrower, the fingers (at least the ones remaining) more well-defined and tapered. At first I thought it was a disease. But there did not appear to be any accompanying weakness. The muscles still appeared taut although diminished in size. There seemed to be a general slowing down.

A special diet came to mind. Low in fat, high in essentials. Perhaps it was health I was observing and not deterioration, which everyone suspected. There are certain stages of each which are difficult to discern, I thought, as I recalled long-distance runners and cyclists, each looking simultaneously malnourished and fit.

But the feeling of agitation and gradual slowness of movement convinced me that a disease had indeed set in. It wasn't a disease with a name or a recognizable constellation of signs and symptoms. Each part of the process simulated a different malady. It was obvious that it was something extraordinary and, though seemingly familiar, like nothing any of us had ever experienced before.

It wasn't AIDS or mid-life crisis or cancer or depression. No one knew what it was. Yet everyone had a solution.

"Eat more meat."

"Chew garlic."

"Exercise hard."

"Stay in bed and rest."

"Seek happiness from within."

"Repent your sins."

"Give more of yourself."

"Look after number one."

Advice flowed as if from the Tower of Babel.

I had my own, but kept it to myself. Nobody really cared. It was all just talk. Worse yet. Nobody even listened. Just chatter and gossip. So things got worse and the sickness grew deeper.

Frustration set in. We didn't need to converse to know it. Hair was pulled from the head and stuffed unhesitantly down the throat. That nearly caused uncontrollable gagging but a self-administered Heimlich maneuver forced the hirsute bolus into the correct conduit. The eyes never flinched; they betrayed nothing. Evidently no harm was done although that act did nothing to solve the affliction. It only produced baldness and a sore throat.

The summer months grew ponderous and oppressive with the heat and blazing sun. One day, sirens pierced the humid air and an ambulance pulled up in front of the house responding to a 911 call. The madness had caused the brutal amputation of both legs. Each of the limbs was seasoned and roasted in methodical, haute culinary fashion. It had taken nearly four weeks to finish, but now only the bones remained for pathology and forensics. Having no legs to stand on, the sickness became prisoner in its own home. The details of what the inside of the house looked like is best left to the imagination.

In the confines of confidential questioning, I learned that the reason given for committing such a ghastly and mutilating deed was that there was a fear that too much energy was being expended to sustain a dwindling life. At least there was an attempt at self-examination. A caloric analysis, crude as it was, determined that the largest group of muscles demanding the most nutrients was in the lower extremities—the human equivalent of the drumstick. It was an inexplicably logical (and correct) conclusion, however misapplied, that by ridding the body of a caloric liability, life might be sustained. It struck me how rational and methodical the reasoning was and this seemed to fit the spirit of the disease's progression. It's hard to argue with logic, no matter how absurd and inappropriate. It was an argument that kept the asylum from permanently adding one more occupant to its expanding numbers.

Knowing the reason why such a drastic action was taken did not lead automatically to a clear understanding of the problem or of the solution. Treatment was intensive for weeks, like most crisis intervention, and then tapered rather quickly as things appeared to revert to normalcy—normal except for the fact that, even as energy was truly conserved by disposing of the legs, movement slowed even further due to the necessity of the special motorized chair. It was sad to see how the appreciation of locomotion dawned only when one became dependent on rolling around aboard a glorified skateboard, symbolically closer to the ground but farther from heaven. Any self-respecting Asian would never allow such self-mutilation. It was disrespectful to one's elders whose spirit resides in the body of each human being. I would have at least realized that the lower extremities are designed in such an efficient manner that to propel oneself with the upper extremities consumes proportionately more energy. Even if I didn't believe in Confucian philosophy, I would have picked a different part of the anatomy—at least stopped at one leg, or better still, just a toe. It was pure stupidity to end up like this.

It was incredible to me that this self-mutilator could not see the obvious deterioration of the body, mind, and, indeed, the soul that accompanied this obsessively voracious behavior. Wasn't there any self-respect? Wasn't there any shame or insight? Wasn't there at least a mirror around? I was drawn to this figure as most people are to things that offend our senses. I felt compelled to follow this oddity one day. The irrationality of it all was mystifying. It was as if I were watching insanity unfold. The curiosity of "how" and "why" prodded me forward.

The pitiful figure attempted to sit upright in the motorized wheelchair, maintaining at least an illusion of respectability and pride. The first stop on this blistering day was the corner mailbox where the wheelchair parked facing the letter slot and waited. The morning passed with the sun rising toward the noon hour and the summer heat sucking the salts and moisture from the body. It never moved.

I was tempted to intervene but had the belief that no one could be so stupid as to sit and watch oneself desiccate while waiting for the mail, even though I wasn't sure that truly was what was happening. And if that was indeed the case, then the poor soul deserved to wither to nothing for believing so much in the reliability of the U.S. Postal Service.

Dogs came by to piss against the leg of the mailbox and to kick up the dirt where they defecated. An elderly couple walked by, six feet and a lifetime apart, without saying a word to the figure or to each other. A mother pulled her child by the arm, cuffing her ear, as the little girl innocently tried to touch the wheelchair. It was haunting to witness this small drama play out in front of me. The surrealism of the players reminded me of the "Twilight Zone" series where peculiar events occur around an unsuspecting, seemingly normal victim. One never knows exactly what is going on, or why, but one knows that something always will. After the little girl left, the poor fellow was alone for another painful ten minutes when something finally did happen.

Three young punks ran up and taunted the figure, flipping the bird with such disregard that I was nearly up to the rescue when the figure at last raised his left arm, stopping the punks dead in their tracks. Instead of swatting at the punks who were close at hand, but still a safe, inaccessible distance from the three-fingered claw, the foreshortened limb went straight to the mouth. The teeth clenched mightily on the thumb, chomping the digit right off at its base, blood jetting into the sky. The punks vomited on the sidewalk. One stumbled back against the mailbox, loosening its legs. The figure then swallowed the thumb whole and began to suck the blood from the stump. The punks took off like birds flushed from their nest while the figure calmly sucked the sanguine juices for nourishment. It was a frighteningly pitiful sight. This parched, decimated creature, sitting alone and abandoned, was draining himself of life like a baby with an empty bottle.

I stood by shaking, not so much from true fright, but because my body did not know whether to upchuck like the punks or yell in disgust at such stupidity. As horrifying as this act was, I kept thinking that this sorry idiot should know that drinking blood, which is high in salt content, will only make a thirst worse. And chewing off a finger to scare off the punks did more injury to himself than the others. More than anything gruesome, I hate stupidity.

I waited for another half an hour, hoping something more dramatic would occur, not because I needed to see more blood and horror, but because there was a delicate balance evident: the calm before the storm versus the calm before the end. I couldn't tell which it was but I wasn't about to upset the balance myself. The stupid fellow just sat there, sucking away.

I was beginning to feel angry and cheated that nothing more was to come of this. This enigma acted so nonchalant. I wanted a denouement here. Now. I began to be annoyed at this charade, bored with this play to nowhere. I came expecting something to happen, and now that something had, I wanted more. I wanted him to die in an epileptic seizure, or raise his hand in a final act of inexplicable mutilation, or even scream for help. Something. Anything. But nothing happened. He slowly took his hand from his mouth, the stump glistening with clot, placed it gently on the control stick of his wheelchair, and moved on.

As the chair rolled down the deserted streets, I looked for a sign of what this creature was thinking, wringing his hands with pain, bowing his head with regret, rolling his eyes with fear. But he remained rigid and fixed to the task at hand, a task only he knew.

I remained a slight distance away, afraid of making visual contact, for I had no idea what my reaction would be if his eyes should meet mine. Perhaps he would cast a malignant spell or pierce my soul with a similar disease or cause me to drown in useless empathy. It was all so irrational. But I wasn't about to take a chance. I was so fearful. So I hid in the background, beyond his shadow.

He finally stopped. I looked at the building he had turned to face. It was no surprise. A hospital. Certainly this was the logical place to turn to for help. Surely he had come to his battered senses and was here to reach out for a cure. A solution seemed so near. But that was not the case.

He sat in the middle of the walkway, staring at the bustling entrance, as humanity with its many faces paraded by. There were the infirm and the frauds, the undeservedly impoverished and the deserving rich. In walked greed and out strolled the generous. People of all races, creeds, beliefs, and conditions. Some were very much alive. Others dead or only half dead. Yet he appeared to all just like them: neither exactly the same, nor entirely different. Each ignored, self-interested, and unpitied in their own right.

I wanted this poor specimen of a human being to wave, yell, bite off his nose, tear off his ear, implore someone to wheel him through the entrance. He seemed so vulnerable yet fearless in his decimated state—directionless yet determined. He was so lost but he also seemed enlightened. I waited, mustering nearly enough courage to push him into the sterile sanctuary. Then I watched, drained of any emotion, as he wheeled himself about and returned home, staining the ground behind him with the blood, still oozing from his wounded hand, hanging limp by his side.

Inexplicably, for days after that, I went through the whole array of human emotions. I had nightmares of sadistic monsters chasing me. I had dreams of healing throughout the world. I felt the rage of destruction and the anger of disempowerment. I felt sadness for the insanity and joy for my own blessed fortitude. I thought of all the hope and happiness which preceded the insanity and the uselessness of a life gone awry; one day wanting to reach out to talk sense into this senselessness, the next wishing this irrational being would devour himself completely.

Thankfully, like most dark hours of life, this state passed, although I was no closer to any truth than before. A few weeks later, I heard a rumor that this poor specter of a soul became so disjointed that he ripped his heart out with his last good hand. It had hurt him so much to do so that he had let out an ungodly, painful scream heard throughout the neighborhood. It was a scream so terrifying that even he couldn't bear the anguish it carried. He had apparently screamed so long and loud that the entire neighborhood came out to see what was happening. The scream continued without a break, yet no one dared to move. No one covered their ears. And no one tried to stop the scream.

Rumor had it that the poor soul couldn't stand it any longer and, in a matter of seconds, in a fit of brilliance or total madness, devoured the rest of his physical body. Then, as a last act of desperation, unable to tolerate the sound of his own wailing, he swallowed his mouth. It was finally quiet and the neighborhood, curious as it was, was so relieved that it turned around and went home, without so much as a yawn.

I didn't believe this rumor, of course, since it was so absurd that believing it would have defined me as being insane as well. But, since that time, no one has seen this crippled character. His body, and definitely his mouth, has never been found. I myself was not inclined to go looking for remnants of such. Thankfully, a seemingly senseless chapter in the history of humankind appeared to have closed with this last bizarre act of self-consumption and stupidity. Even then, I had my doubts.

You see, halfway through life, I know that nothing really dies. Things only change. And the most important thing is to change for the better. But somewhere in the universe—in fact, everywhere—the spirit of the fool lives on. That final scream of pain continues to shatter every moment of silence even though I, like many, may not always hear it and may not ever heed it. You cannot stop the scream or the pain by swallowing the mouth. That is merely stupid. That is not the real source. You can only stop the scream by biting your fingernails if you have to. But only the fingernails. Nothing more.

15

You <u>Can</u> Take It with You

I hate shopping. I think it is one of the biggest wastes of human time along with sleeping in past nine and blow-drying your hair. If you critically look at all the items you buy, very few are absolutely necessary. The clutter in any basement and attic will attest to that.

You need light bulbs and batteries, orange juice and bread, a bed and toothpaste, a few good books, toilet paper, and probably a car. But you really don't need an electric meat carver, silk underwear, or a TV set in every single room of the house—all of which I have.

When you get right down to it, what we shop for are either things we need or things we desire, or at least *think* we need or desire at the time of the purchase. Sometimes we have a preset goal of what we want, like buying a black Range Rover or dating a tall blonde. At other times, we wander around aimlessly, as if at a college mixer, waiting to be inspired, until it is one o'clock in the morning and we have yet to find that elusive possession we feel we must have, but cannot clearly describe.

I must admit that most of my purchases in life have been made of necessity, such as the biweekly forays to the local grocery store to replenish my nearly empty refrigerator or the triennial excursion to the men's store to rejuvenate my outdated and frayed wardrobe. The decision between chicken thighs or T-bone steak is not very monumental when one's belly is empty, and choosing brown pants over beige is not too taxing when the whites of one's underwear is beginning to show through the crotch. But when I find myself shopping for unnecessary items, especially expensive ones, I need to be inspired before laying out my credit card.

The value people seek in shopping or possessing can be measured in terms of time, such as, what will give us immediate, or near immediate, pleasure—thus the carton of orange juice. At the other extreme are the desirable things that will give us long-lasting joy and happiness—thus, the spouse. The former items are fairly easy to spring for because of their immediacy or urgency. It is the latter investments that are more difficult because they require us to look at longevity, not only of the purchase, but also of the purchaser.

Yesterday, I spent three hours wandering through eight of the most fashionable and trendy furniture stores along Decorator's Row. I was hunting for a bedroom set, a dining room combo, and a coffee table. Now none of these was absolutely necessary since I already had a functional bedroom and dining room ensemble, even if they were quite inexpensive, old, and unmatched. Likewise, I really didn't need a two-thousand-dollar coffee table on which to put my seventy-five-cent cup of coffee or even my fifty-dollar art books. And I know that once I buy that coffee table, my wife would never let me rest my weary but filthy feet on it. So who needs it?

Yet I knew that these were purchases I would have to make at some time if I wanted to maintain my dignity and domestic tranquility. You can only live like a student or bachelor for so long. The trouble was, I didn't know exactly what I wanted. Like most people, I can more easily tell what I don't like than what I do. So, true to the pure art of living, I waited for inspiration to strike.

I thought about what items in my house I value the most and would attempt to save in the event of a disaster such as an earthquake or fire, both very real possibilities in L.A. I suppose the first thing, besides my spouse since she's close at hand in the next room, would be my violins, each of which I have had since my teens and are fine Italian instruments over two hundred years old. Both have sentimental value, but also possess an artistry and craftsmanship which will last long after my death. So, too, my modest art collection. An immeasurable amount of talent, inventiveness, and soul went into making these treasures and these are the very qualities I hold important to life. Other than these, only the things connected to my past seem worth saving. I couldn't care less about my silk underwear and espresso machine which I don't even know how to run. I could always buy a new leather sofa and big-screen television; Los Angeles is overrun with leather and televisions. Similarly, all the food in the refrigerator and freezer will spoil before my next birthday. They are unquestionably expendable and quite easily replaced. I can't really see myself running out of a burning house with a frozen turkey under one arm and a quart of milk under the other. Nothing in the refrigerator is worth risking life or limb for, except perhaps the frozen remnant of my wedding cake which my wife and I keep for some obscure tradition or superstition.

As the afternoon wore on, I became more and more glassy-eyed while searching for all this furniture. In shopping, I was continually reminded of my mortality, my transientness. I was shown tables of aluminum and mahogany, granite and glass. Chairs of leather and stained ash. Coffee tables of travertine, dyed suede under polyurethane lacquer, marble, and brass. The choices and workmanship were staggering. But it was not a question of how durable these beautiful and well-made pieces of furniture were. They would certainly last longer than me. It was a question of how long I would have to enjoy them. Would I soon move to a house sporting a different style? Would I change my outlook and tastes? Would I even die before I got my money's worth of enjoyment? Coupled with the fact that none of these pieces in the eight stores inspired me, it is not surprising why I thought shopping that day was such a waste and that I had just spent three hours of my precious life for naught. No wonder most men do not understand a woman's need to shop. Waiting for inspiration to strike so I can buy an unnecessary piece of furniture was a kind of double whammy of useless paralysis. Nothing was compelling enough for me to act. In the meanwhile, I felt very foolish and impotent.

This afternoon would not have been unlike the many other weekend afternoons I have spent shopping for unnecessary things except for an enlightening encounter with a breast cancer patient the day before. That consultation began like the hundreds of other conversations with breast reconstruction patients. She was a pleasant, dignified woman of sixty-two, outgoing, but modest in personality. She spoke intelligently and rationally about her discovery of the cancer. And she knew enough of herself to know that she wanted to have breast reconstruction. Her life was *not* going to fall apart if she could help it.

First, I spent a significant amount of time gaining *her* perspective of her disease and *her* expectations. I asked how she came to discover the cancer. Was she diligent and disciplined enough to have performed monthly self-examinations or was she a reluctant subject screened by mammography? Did she take this disease in stride like so many of life's trials or was this an unthinkable, unmentionable horror?

I tried to get a sense of her self-image. What kind of clothes did she wear? Did she want to change her breast size or shape? How did she feel about her "good" breast? Was her breast an integral part of her identity or merely an unnecessary but desirable appendage?

I wanted to know about her support system. Who was in her family? What did her husband feel about her disease and her body?

I needed to know her level of tolerance and expectation. Did she have an opinion about the much-maligned silicone breast prostheses? Did she want the best result regardless of the nature and number of surgeries? What about scars? What warranty would she accept and what complications could she endure?

I presented her with the entire array of options for reconstruction: immediate or delayed, prosthetic or autogenous (using her own tissues), single or multistaged. We reviewed controversies associated with artificial prostheses. We discussed location of scars for the different varieties of flaps used to recreate the breast mound. We explored different combinations of surgeries to achieve a variety of end results. I felt as if I had given her as much knowledge and insight as any good "sales consultant" should.

Finally, we settled on immediate reconstruction in two stages using autogenous tissue from her abdomen. Since her new breast would be made from her own muscle, fat and skin, without a silicone prosthesis, it was living tissue. It wouldn't rupture, disintegrate, erode, or melt. It would effectively last as long as she did.

We were now in a surgical marriage; it is something you enter into reluctantly, but with eventual certainty and confidence, with someone you trust beyond all others to carry you through both the good times and, especially, the potentially bad times. We were all set to go.

Unfortunately, this patient had just changed her insurance company to a managed care plan and, thus, had become a captive of that system. With managed care (which to some extent is really managed *non*care), the patient is put in the untenable position of not being able to shop for what she wants. It is like requiring a person to live in a house where all the furniture is brass and glass just because one bought a brass and glass coffee table. Or, imagine that, having procured a Macy's charge card, you are now not permitted to shop at Neiman Marcus, or if you eat at McDonald's you are not allowed into Burger King. To me, this loss of freedom is distinctly un-American.

During our followup conversation, I explained how my hands were tied by her health care plan since I was not contracted with them. She was contractually off-limits to me. I tried gently to release her from my care. I suggested other doctors in her plan. I down-played my expertise and experience. But to her, we were already married and she would have none of this talk about divorce, amicable as it might be. She had decided to have me do her reconstruction even if it meant paying for it out of her own pocket. She was sold and she wanted that new breast. Having no plans to be dissuaded, she said something that many people say in times of insight and conviction: "We're not paupers and we're not rich. But I know what I want. I want *you* to operate on me. I don't care what it costs because it's my life and I can't take it with me."

I was both flattered and astonished that she had such confidence in me. Was it because of her referring surgeon's recommendations? I hoped it was because of my reputation and our rapport, but perhaps it had more to do with a sense of defiance against such an unjust and restrictive system. That she was willing to go out on such a financial limb reminded me of the intangible and fast-fading benefits of medical practice: an indescribable feeling of satisfaction when another human being confides an unconditional trust in *your* judgment and *your* abilities, and not only because they are forced to. That she could be so unflaggingly confident in her own decision immediately won my respect.

In reaching her decision, she was measuring her own mortality, prioritizing her own desires. Breast cancer at sixty-two is not at all like having unmatched furniture at thirty-nine. This is where decisions of needs and desires were crucial. No prolonged agony of traipsing around to eight different surgeons of mammary fashion. No time to waste on being inspired. No self-doubts.

Yet this purchase of a new breast wasn't something everyone would consider necessary. It wasn't the same as a new heart valve to replace a

diseased valve or a radial tire to replace a flat. It would come under the
heading of, say, very desirable furniture: functional, reasonable, aesthetic, perhaps a reflection of one's own personality. But not absolutely
necessary for survival. It was the stunning glass and granite dining room
set I was looking for and couldn't yet find to replace my current wobbly
wooden one.

I was thinking of asking this wonderfully brave and inspired woman
to do my shopping for me. She seemed to absorb all the details, articu-
late her desires, juxtapose her relative mortality, and synthesize a decision. She had the inspiration and conviction to act. She wasn't wasting
her time. Hopefully, she wasn't wasting her money either. I needed someone like that to decorate my house.

I say that with self-deprecating cynicism. Next to her decision, mine
should be a cinch. There are times I take life seriously and times I
shouldn't, and most of the time they are one and the same, like trying to
decide which cereal to buy or which toothpaste to use. You can spend
hours staring at cereal boxes.

We all have different approaches to shopping. To shop is to know the
secrets of your soul. Just look at people next time you go to the grocery
store.

Like this patient, I, too, used to believe that you can't take it with
you—not necessarily just money, but real things. The ancient Egyptians
believed otherwise and buried pets, slaves and spouses with the dead. So,
too, do practicing Buddhists who are forever burning cold hard currency
so the deceased can use it in heaven or wherever good Buddhists go. But
the point of the expression is well taken. If you have the dough, blow it.
The choice is between dough and no dough. Things or nothing. Your
mother told you you can't have everything. She was right, so don't worry
about it. Shopping, when faced with death and disease, is all of a sudden
a pretty fatalistic, self-limiting act. Go for it. It's not all that important in
the big scheme of life and death, and you won't be able to carry it with
you to your grave. I doubt if any dining room table, no matter how gor-
geous and solidly constructed, would fit into any coffin when I get laid
six feet under.

But it struck me that afternoon after returning empty-handed and dis-
heartened, while resting my weary, but filthy, feet on the leather sofa because I had no coffee table handy, that my clever and courageous patient

had truly found a way to shopping heaven. For in her desire to proceed with the reconstruction of her new breast, made from her own precious flesh and blood and designed to last a lifetime, no matter what happened between now and forever, turning task into triumph, she had decided that she *could* have it all. Necessary or not, she *can* take it with her when she goes.

And she will.

Smart shopper.

16

Vision

Paddling about in amniotic fluid during our early life, we cannot see anything. A film covers our eyes like a veil and we are content with the dark warm ignorance of the watery womb. Blinded by boredom, lulled into lethargy, we also have nothing to see. As a fetus, our eyesight need not be (and isn't) much better than that of a baby guppy.

When we finally emerge from the uterus, into the lively and colorful world of life, vision plays an invaluable role in shaping our lives. At first, our brain registers crude, nondescript images as the rods and cones of the retina are bombarded with new stimuli. It will be months before anything meaningful gets transferred into our stream of consciousness. Then, we merely blink reflexively to light or its movement. After a while, we begin to track objects with increasing curiosity. A bit later, we come to understand what different light impulses stand for. One means green, another is called red. A third means it's time to get up. It is only many years later that we truly understand the *value* in interpreting all these light impulses.

For the first few years of life, much of these light impulses were just images to which I reacted as a basic, animalistic reflex, such as "chopsticks approaching with food, open mouth and swallow" or "ball rolling across floor, move limbs frantically like fish fins" or "wall ahead, smash skull into said wall to prove concept of immobility and definition of solid state." This last one required slightly more advanced thought processing.

Beyond such immediate reactions, vision was relatively noncognitive. It was something I took for granted. We all do. The same was true for breathing and eating. In fact, the first memory of vision is one of *not* being able to see, which is often the case with things we take for granted.

I rarely failed anything back then. But I did fail my eye exam. My optometrist didn't have any of the fancy optical equipment available today. It was simply the old-fashioned letter chart on the wall, not even the one with the arrows for those inclined to memorize the letter chart. I didn't get much beyond E and the next two or three lines. So I was fitted with thick glasses at a very early age. I hated them because no one else had to wear such ridiculous-looking objects on their face. The glasses were a nuisance: fogging up in cold weather, fogging up in hot weather, falling off my nose from their weight when I sweat. My parents and sister had perfect vision, but I needed glasses because my performance in the eye exam was so pathetic. My glasses just got thicker and thicker as I grew older and older and I flunked more and more eye exams. I was afraid they'd get so thick, I'd reach the limits of optical technology and it would be physically impossible to wear them. There must be a limit to the weight a nose can withstand. As such, myopia changed my whole life.

■ ■ ■

Glasses became a necessary tool for all of life's challenges, while carrying their own burden of geekiness. I needed them to hit a baseball. I needed them to read music. I needed them just to eat peas. Having to wear these heavy glass coasters was so bad that the times when I had to tape a broken hinge or wipe spaghetti sauce off the front face or retrieve a pair knocked cock-eyed through my football helmet scarred me for life. I hated not being able to see.

I'm sure that most young kids who have to wear glasses feel very self-conscious and either submit to its emasculation or overcompensate with aggressiveness. I was one of the former who spent much of the time hiding behind that wall of glass. Just as people see others who wear obtrusive objects on their noses in a certain light, so, too, do those who have to view the world through a glass barrier or suffer the consequences of not seeing at all. Unlike truly blind people who cannot see another's reaction to them, people like me, who wear glasses in order to see others, can very much see their reactions. These reactions color our world.

Not all reactions have to be obvious and dramatic. Like fish, I easily sensed subtle changes in my environment. One thing I noticed when wearing glasses was that I acted as if I had one layer of insulation between me and the rest of the world. It felt like the real world of life was being played out on a screen attached to my glasses, giving me a detached, objective point of view. I was above it all, looking down or in, one-way observation. I often did not truly feel as if I were a part of the real world, but rather a voyeur of sorts. I could play with friends and still have this awkward feeling as if I really didn't belong. I could participate in debates or arguments, throw out provocative barbs, and not fear being hurt in retaliation. It was life behind a bullet-proof screen.

Another thing I noticed was that even with my glasses on, my vision, although corrected to 20/20, never seemed perfect. Things were never as crystal clear as you expect things to be at that age. One eye may be slightly out of focus compared to the other. The glasses may be a bit tilted on the nose so that I wasn't looking straight out the center of one lens. When out in the sunlight playing sports, the glare from the sun or the jiggling when I ran distorted my vision.

I adjusted to these situations in a number of ways which I have only recently realized. I became more aware of everything around me—in effect, expanding my field of vision to help my brain see. For instance, I might not have been able to follow the fast-moving squash ball, but I could be facing the front wall, my opponent behind me, and know exactly where he was, what type of stroke he was using, and thus anticipate where the ball was going. Awareness and anticipation became natural, allowing me to coalesce a large array of semifocused stimuli into a cohesive impression and understanding. I had a good net game in tennis largely because of the ability to "read" my opponent and anticipate. It is not unlike knowing what a person will say before he says it because of all the extraneous, subconscious signals he projects. I feel, therefore I see.

The other thing I noticed was that I became a skeptic. When you don't know if what you are seeing is really what you are seeing, you have to exclude the things it can't be. What others took as obvious truth, I questioned; not because I didn't believe in it or understand it, but because psychologically I didn't always believe what my eyes saw and, by then, I sensed there was a whole other side of life than what was directly in front of my eyes. I forced people, and myself, to the point of exasperation, to question what appeared to be obvious. A simple statement of presumed fact—the sky is blue—brought forth a whole litany of alternatives stretching reason and patience.

No, it's turning gray.

It's partly cloudy.

It's not as blue as it is back east.

Is it really blue or just the ocean's reflection?

How blue is blue and what exactly is blue?

What do you mean by blue?

Blah, blah, blah. . . .

You get the point. All this skepticism turned me into a perfectionist (and a pain in the ass to some) and forced me to understand all I could about everything. This didn't mean I always did understand, but at least I tried, tried to really "see."

All this took place when my vision was corrected. When I took my glasses off, the world became a total blur. I was literally disconnected from my environment visually. A car could be moving right in front of me and I wouldn't know it until I was on the ground in pain from the impact. I couldn't catch a bouncing beach ball or even see the beach. My vision was so bad that I knew I could get out of being drafted during the Vietnam years. Fortunately my number came up three hundred sixty-something out of 365 so I didn't have to carry around all the guilt of a medical exemption or the guilt of failing combat.

This lack of vision saved me and scores of others. Imagine if I lost my glasses during a military confrontation. I'd be a danger to everyone around me. Since I wouldn't be able to relate to my surroundings, I wouldn't know just how big a danger I was. It'd be like hiding from "It" in Hide-and-Seek. If you hid behind a tree and, by keeping your head buried in the bark, you couldn't see "It," you always assumed that "It" couldn't see you. What a surprise when you were found crouching behind a six-inch tree trunk! Vietnam was a bad enough war without having nearsighted soldiers running into each other in the rice paddies or worrying that a little mud on their lenses was the difference between being a hero and coming home in a pine box.

On the other hand, it is a peculiar sensation to be so isolated. That is where vision really failed me. As my nearsightedness grew worse, my glasses grew thicker and my sense of isolation grew more pronounced. Sometimes it was as if I were living life through the television screen; that is, watching things happen, experiencing events, but not being able to truly touch those around me, as if it were all make-believe. It was in large part due to my lack of clear vision and those infernal glasses. People reacted to the glasses and not to the person behind them. Or so I thought.

I soon longed for old age, during which I had heard that farsightedness would set in. I would self-correct my poor vision and toss away my glasses, free to experience an unfiltered world. I couldn't wait for that time in life when everything that was now blurred beyond a foot of my cornea would finally be clear.

There is another side to this. The ability to take off my glasses and "leave" my environment by making everything blurred improved my innate sensitivity to the world of intangibles. I could turn the screen off at any time. I would often play my violin in my small and private world defined by a twelve-inch zone of clear vision surrounding me. By shutting out everything else, I got in touch more easily with the feeling of the music. As such, a whole new world came alive with sound and emotion. No wonder that many musicians play best, and with most genuine sensitivity, when they close their eyes completely and play straight from the heart. It is a revelation to be able to sink so completely into an exclusive sensation. It's like meditation.

Although I do not perform surgery without corrective lenses, I often close one eye and squint through the other. Blurring my vision enough when I exam a patient or assess my work on the operating table, I get a better artistic sense of form and proportion than when details are glaringly obvious and distracting. Reality becomes more evident when you aren't influenced only by what you see, but also by what you don't see. Truth isn't defined only by what is said, but also by what is left unsaid. Then again, I might have developed the habit because I've always seen artists in front of their models and easels, holding up their thumb and squinting through one eye. At least, that's what I think I saw. Whatever. It works.

There were many times when, overcome with sadness or loneliness, I withdrew even further from the tangible world by removing my glasses and "fogging out." When people were around who tormented me by their mere presence, like old flames and male competitors, not being able to see them made me feel more comfortable and protected. The lack of sight then becomes a convenient form of escapism.

By eliminating the distractions of sight, insights come more easily. Perhaps that's why people tend to look upward at nothing in particular or shut their eyes tightly when trying to think. We contemplate with our minds, not our eyes.

■   ■   ■

Some of these feelings changed when I graduated from high school, not because I was any less sensitive, but because I was so sensitive that I got contact lenses. I couldn't bear the thought of going through college wearing pop bottle bottoms on my face. Like most contact wearers, I had to suffer through two weeks of unbelievable self-torture feeling as if someone were sticking forks into my eyeballs and twisting them. My eyes looked red and inflamed, tears streaming down my chubby cheeks. I sniffled. I sneezed. I suffered. I probably made those around me feel just as miserable as I was. But ask any contact wearer and they'll say it's all worth it. I certainly would. I looked better. I read better. I played sports better. I think I made love better. I earned it with every tear I shed.

One thing I couldn't do anymore was hide. I no longer had that sense of a barrier between me and the rest of the world. I couldn't whip off my glasses and blur that relationship. Words no longer had to penetrate a pane of glass to reach my brain and what I saw when I peered out at the world around me was not a reflection of light, but the real thing. Most importantly, other people could see me and not a reflection of themselves in my thick-lensed glasses.

For the first seventeen years, I couldn't get away from glasses. For the next seventeen, I didn't even own a pair. I was totally dependent on my contact lenses. I was such a foolish person that even when I lost one lens, like the time I fell into the hotel swimming pool in Kauai, I preferred to walk around half-disoriented and out of focus than buy a cursed pair of glasses.

When I fell asleep tending those late night shifts during residency, my lens would be firmly attached to my eyeball so that the act of awakening became a feared event. I would have to pry open my lids and peel the lens off my cornea like ripping skin from the flesh of my face. There was no question I was envious of people who had perfect vision. As much as contact lenses corrected my vision and improved my lot in life, I couldn't wait for my vision to reverse itself from nearsightedness to far-sightedness. Ever since I knew my eyesight, bad as it was, would exempt me from military duties, I lived under the presumption that far-vision improved with age. I couldn't wait to age. I wanted to be normal.

■   ■   ■

And then it happened. I remember the day so well since it gave me such an eye-opening jolt. I was sitting on the toilet as I did every morning of the week. Directly in front of the toilet I have a magazine bin with dozens of magazines and throwaway catalogues that seem to miraculously appear in my mailbox every week. I thought at first that my lenses weren't clean or that I had mistakenly switched the left with the right. Maybe I didn't have enough lens solution in. Maybe I had too much. I rubbed my eyes. I blinked a few times to clear the lenses. Nothing seemed to help. Try as I might, I couldn't clearly see the half clad models in the *Victoria's Secret* catalogue!

You see, this catalogue comes every few weeks. Every guy in America with a girlfriend or wife seems to have a few copies lying around. You don't even need to subscribe. They just come. Miraculously. Thankfully. I even use it in my consultations with cosmetic patients, especially prior to breast surgery. I'm so familiar with this catalogue that, usually, I can recognize the different models. Each one has her own distinctive feature. One with the oversized lips. Another with the overdone nose. A third with the overflowing bosom.

This morning, I couldn't see any of them clearly enough to distinguish one from the other. I nearly jumped up to wash out my eyes until I realized that I was still on the toilet. So I blinked and squinted and closed one eye, then the other, and blinked again. No matter what I did, my vision was the same.

I gradually moved the catalogue up and down, back and forth. Unlike before, whenever I moved the page closer, things got more blurred. When I moved it further away, I recognized the models. It was then that I realized I had become farsighted. Great! I'm losing my nearsightedness. No more glasses! No more contact lenses! I'll soon live a normal life.

It took another ten seconds before it dawned on me. My elation fell to despair and sadness. I felt all my muscles go slack and just stared without focus at this page of bathing beauties. What I thought from the beginning of adolescence would be a joyous occasion had become another affirmation of my mortality and of the unrelenting march toward the inevitable. The far-sightedness which was to have compensated for my nearsightedness and made me whole, was, in reality, presbyopia, a *sign of aging*. I was stunned.

I sat on that toilet for an extraordinary amount of time. Neither my body nor my bowels could move. Overnight, I had become a member of the elderly, passing from self-conscious adolescent to self-conscious aged. As I moved the catalogue further and further away from my face, I envisioned myself with the obligatory bifocals, head thrown back, eyes squinting, eruditely and wisely scrutinizing bras, bikinis, and bustiers. No! This couldn't be happening so soon!

But it was. The clarity of the models' features lying near my crumpled pajama bottoms so close to the floor confirmed this fact. I felt cheated. I was dejected. Life was not supposed to turn out like this.

For the next few weeks, I became more and more conscious of the presbyopia, cursing the aging process that it harbingered and anticipating the improvement in vision that never came. Presbyopia, in fact, did not bring the ability to see far objects which I thought farsightedness would, but took away the ability to see near objects—the only vision I had! I still had to stick things under my nose to read when I didn't have my contacts in, but also had to adjust for the inability to focus on near print when I did have them in. The *Victoria's Secret* catalogue gradually ended up around my ankles. It was the worst of both worlds.

I spent so many years with my nose literally buried in a book or magazine that retraining myself to read at arm's length continually reminded me of the frailties of my life. Just as the need to live life peering through a thick glass window influenced my behavior, so did this need to adjust to my newfound presbyopia. Not only were menus in dim-lit romantic restaurants impossible to read, but the peas on the plate were blurred once again. Any time I leaned close enough to kiss someone, I immediately got dizzy trying to focus on their face.

■   ■   ■

Since that time on the toilet, I admit I have looked at my life a little differently. I curse the minutes that tick on and the vision which never seems any better. Yet, insecurities don't bother me as much. What I look like in glasses worries me less than whether I can see at all. And whether I can see at all is less important than what I do or think once I've seen whatever there is to see. There is more to life than just eyeballs, although I admit that I would still rather wear contacts than glasses.

I am more forward-looking, although you may not realize it by reading this book. This is not because I expect to see any better in the future, but because there is a realization that some things will happen no matter how you protect yourself and no matter how much you expect it not to happen. And there is nothing you can do to stop it.

Maybe that's why fetuses are so content. Things are going to develop the way they are. There is no use worrying over whether or not the primitive film over your eyes is going to regress or if you'll ever get out of this dark, watery cavern alive. Before you know it, life as a fetus will end, out you come, and suddenly the light seems so very bright.

I know one day I will have to give in and purchase a set of reading glasses. In my usual stubborn way, I will have put this off until I surrender completely even though I know I will have to eventually. I understand that. I envision buying that first pair of reading glasses. It will be diopter 1.00, the lowest. I'll think: How ironic and cruel! Instead of *not* having to wear contact lenses and glasses in my old age, I'll have to wear *both* in order to see.

I will accept it by then. But not because I expect to see any better, although I know I will. And not because I will look any better, because I won't. But because then I will know that I have seen much of life. More than most. More than I ever could imagine as a fat, geeky kid with thick pop-bottle-bottom glasses living in a neighborhood of four or five houses and playing in a field called the Pit. And because I will be destined and eager to see more—yet in a decidedly and expectedly different way. Because that which I see will be like nothing I've seen before. What I've never seen I will want to understand. And what I understand I will then love. For the next half of my life, that is my vision.

See?

17

Half Dead

It has been years since, peering into the bureau mirror of my little boy's room, I noticed how thin my hair had become. I admit that that one solitary image shocked me to the point of all-consuming fear. It's only natural. Perhaps half dead then, I am now certainly that and probably more. Now whenever I look into a mirror and see the receding hairline, the early jowls, and the tired eyes, I tell myself optimistically, but not always successfully, "Cheer up . . . you're only *half* dead!"

Much has changed ever since that revealing day. I have relived my entire childhood with these writings. I have gained a few more pounds and lost more than a few additional strands of that precious hair. I have given up a loyal girlfriend and won a steadfast, albeit at times trying, wife. I have seen dreams fade and the future become my past. I have diminished sight but clearly enhanced insight. I have taken a few more unrelenting steps toward the inevitable. I am more than half dead, rounding second, and heading for home. And I am more scared than ever.

Recently, in addition to a multitude of both natural and unnatural disasters to hit southern California, the area I now call home was traumatized by a devastating earthquake and all of its equally traumatizing aftershocks. During this vulnerable time, I felt very little of the fear and anxiety others were feeling. For some reason, the unpredictability and defenselessness of it all left me with a calming sense of fatalism, while for others, this gave rise to a paralyzing terror. For me, there was even a perverse sense of excitement, something happening to break up the monotonous routine of everyday life.

The 6.8 quake came out of the dark and innocent silence of early morning sleep with the suddenness and fury of a fifty-car freight train that threw my wife and me out of our bed onto the trembling floor. We landed on a large painting which had come crashing to the floor in a shower of glass, barely missing our heads on its way down. The house felt as if it were about to explode and the terrifying thunder of noise all around convinced me that the structure had already done so. The joints screamed and glass and china smashed onto the hardwood floor. Joanne and I grabbed each other in a stranglehold, as we never had before, awaiting our inevitable end at the bottom of the canyon. We held on as if riding out the meanest and angriest tempest—each fierce rocking giving rise to yet another tremor. I was thankful for each living second that passed. The shaking finally ended, as we knew it would, one way or another.

We stumbled safely to the front of the house and spent the next two hours huddled obediently in the entrance doorway, each attempt to reenter the house prompting an eerie aftershock, keeping us "imprisoned" outdoors. The earth seemed to know how to tame us humans. It was truly a humbling experience. That day and the ones to follow were spent contemplating fate and coping with fear and the frightening expectation that the Big One was yet to come.

Partly because her personality demanded compartmentalization and orderliness, and mostly because of her paranoia (which wasn't necessarily or entirely imagined), Joanne undertook the task of preparing for the Big One which many decreed to be imminently forthcoming. Innumerable trips to the grocery store and local hardware supply shop saw our house ladened with case upon case of bottled mountain spring water (why one needed to import water from a country twelve thousand miles away still puzzles me); packages of freeze-dried Japanese cuisine such as chicken yakitori and beef teriyaki (a real hit with all those Japanese camping enthusiasts); no fewer than *eight* flashlights (one for each room of the house); a battery-powered nightlight for every unoccupied outlet (making our house glitter like a Christmas window display); an emergency escape ladder to toss out of our bedroom window (which would seem quite unnecessary if our second-story bedroom were to collapse right down to the ground floor); a crowbar under the bed with which to pry open a jammed door (or to bash in an unwanted intruder's skull if he or she had the gall and energy to hike the mile and a half up an isolated canyon ridge to our unprotected house), along with chains, bolts, screws, and quake wax to secure anything that could possibly move (my suggestion of nailing our ever-ready sneakers to the floor next to the bed wasn't taken very kindly); and, finally, a sturdy, plastic, flaming-yellow construction hardhat (which I couldn't decide was to be used for rummaging through the crumbled aftermath or worn during dinner while waiting for the destructive foremath). I'm sure all this is prudent preparation for the inevitable and she should be commended and even leased out to others for this purpose. But fear was obviously a major motivating factor, so I pressed her on this issue, albeit gently and diplomatically.

"What are you *really* afraid of?" I asked.

She seemed annoyed at such a trivial and obvious question, answering without so much as a whit of self-consciousness or doubt. "I'm not afraid of dying. I don't care if I'm crushed. I just don't want to be buried alone."

What courageous cowardice! She didn't seem to mind getting crushed under a three-story heap of rubble. She just didn't want to be the only one at that time.

Dying itself was not the issue. She was most afraid of getting caught alone in our canyon house, which she now calls the "Death Trap," and she was especially afraid of the kitchen, now dubbed the "Hell Hole." She talked of the projected eight minutes of shaking, the thirteen-foot-high pile of broken glass in the downtown high-rise district, and the innumerable obstacles to boarding a nonstop flight at LAX to the safe and sunny beaches of Hawaii. It dawned on me that all those forementioned supplies were intended to allow her to survive long enough, or to escape easily enough, to join up with someone with whom she could happily, fearlessly, perhaps even willingly, die. Undoubtedly someone like me. She wasn't about to let the phrase "till death us do part" stand in her fearful way.

None of this succeeded in convincing me to accept her particular level of fear. But it did make me think of what it is that I most feared. Was it truly death or just the fear of growing old? It was neither, for those were inevitable. Instead, I feared losing the love for life itself; losing that thrill of Fenway Park because of greed; losing the joy of music-making because of diminishing ability; losing the desire for medical practice because of law, politics, and market forces.

I looked at her fear and saw how it overtook her life. I felt a sorrow (after I had a good laugh about the oversized hardhat) because this wasn't how life was intended—to be preoccupied with death and dying; consumed by fear, insecurity, anger, and frustration. Life was for the living!

Perhaps that is why so many people are innately destructive. They have little to live for. They don't lament the fact that they are losing hair or need reading glasses. They don't care about their potbellies or the fact that they can't remember nursery rhymes. They don't care if they've accomplished anything or learned anything about themselves. Some of them can't wait to die just to be rid of life. Those people are afraid of *not* dying. I'm afraid of not living.

■　　■　　■

Someone had said that it is not how old you are that's important. It's how much time you have left. One never knows how long that is—even if you're on death row or living in "The Death Trap." That is what causes the fear as much as the uncertainty of when the Big One is going to strike. The irony of the paradox—you remember Zeno's paradox?—is that not only can you not reach the destination because of the infinite halfway points along the way, but that you can't even tell when you are halfway there. That happens only when you get to wherever it is you are going. And then, it doesn't matter any more.

I have asked myself how I would live life differently if I had known how much time I had left. It is a little presumptuous of me to think that under that hypothetically unpleasant situation, I would think as rationally as I do now. Still, I think I can answer that with some truth as some people at some stage in their life unfortunately must.

I have treated challenges in my life as if they were my only challenges without pretending or knowing that they might truly be my last. That is, the exams I took starting in nursery school, when I was separated from the rest of the class to work on math problems in an isolated corner of the room, I took without the presumption that I could retake them if I failed or that I would be forgiven a mistake just because I was so young. The recitals I played as a fledgling violinist were played with all the seriousness and nervousness of a final performance, but without my knowing that one day I might never be able to draw the horse-haired bow across the steel-woven strings with anything remotely resembling good harmony. Every swing of the bat and every toss of the baseball were made with the inspiration of the major leaguer I once imagined I was but never became. Each operation, even each small element of every operation, was accomplished with the ultimate and sole interest of that most important patient's well-being in mind without presumption or belief that I had any influence over the way that patient really faced life. It was rare that I took today for granted in favor of tomorrow.

When I was five, I never thought beyond six. When I was ten, I had no idea what twenty would be like. And when I was twenty, thirty was still way out there. I hardly ever thought about my past or dreamed of the distant future. I was too busy living to be worried about dying.

So in all good conscience, I can admit that my life has been lived as if I were *always* half dead, yet even then, full of life. It's just that I never looked or felt the part. Now that I do, at least occasionally, and usually when I'm tired and stark naked, the task ahead is to convince myself that life is *not* half over or even half begun or just a prelude to an everlasting afterlife somewhere high up in nirvana or in some heavenly Episcopalian paradise, but that it is just as mysterious, wondrous, fresh, innocent, and, yes, even fearfully challenging as it was the day I was born when I had less hair than now and proportionately more body fat, when I couldn't run or crawl, had fewer dreams, a weaker memory, poorer vision, no past and an uncertain future.

Half-dead . . . it ain't so bad after all.